Praise for *Becom*
Business Manager

"Before starting my business I had spent more than 25 years working corporate jobs leading and managing teams specializing in finance, sales, marketing, HR, and administration. I wanted to be able to work at home while my kids were in middle and high school, so I decided to open my own VA (type) business. I say "type" because I didn't really want to be a virtual assistant and help people with tasks, I wanted to partner with my clients and help them lead and grow their businesses. I was struggling with the "time for money" trap and the ebbs and flows of too much, or not enough, work and I was not working with my ideal clients either. I was struggling to make enough money to support my family.

When I found the book, *Becoming an Online Business Manager*, I was so excited to know there was a term for what I was! It gave me great insights into the skills I needed to have and that I could skip being a VA altogether. My advice for anyone thinking of becoming an OBM is DON'T WAIT. I put off investing in the Certified OBM training and struggled for another year. I wish I had done it sooner and saved myself that year of stress. I love being an OBM and I know so many more people can be

successful in this career and business who are leaving or want to leave their corporate jobs. I am grateful every day for finding this book. It opened up so many more opportunities for me and business."
Keldie Jamieson, Certified OBM Trainer

"I considered myself a pretty high-level virtual assistant who was already in the six-figure range, but I felt I had hit the ceiling on what I could charge my clients and how I could help them. I knew I could do more for my clients, but I wasn't sure what that looked like or how I could get away from the "dollars for hours" grind. My VA practice was in the perfect position to revamp and switch to Online Business Manager mode and I loved the concept of base pay and incentives. I know I can do anything and move my practice in any direction that I want to. I have all the tools I need to really accelerate growth in my practice, make a bigger impact for my clients and have fun doing it! I highly recommend *Becoming an Online Business Manager* -- it changed my life!"
Sharon Broughton, Certified OBM Trainer

"I started my virtual service business in 2008 with one goal in mind: to work from home. I just wanted to be home with my then 1st and 4th grader... little did I know where the journey would take me. I started out as a

Virtual Assistant, anything a business owner didn't want to deal with I just started doing... from editing eBooks to building web pages. Every day was a new something to learn, to conquer. However, it didn't take long before I realized that I had a passion to play a much bigger role in my clients' businesses. I was super annoyed with inefficiencies. I could see clearly what needed to be done but because I was viewed as an 'assistant' by my clients they couldn't hear my suggestions. I was in a box... and I was not loving that box. I knew I had something more to offer, but I had no idea what or how to make that happen. Until I received a copy of Tina's book *Becoming an Online Business Manager*.

I remember a Sunday afternoon sitting on the chaise in my living room with my husband watching a movie while I read the book. Literally, I had tears in my eyes as I looked at him and said: "This is what I was meant to do, what I was created to do". (Yes, I am pretty passionate that way... a life on purpose means something to me.) That started the journey... to stepping into my true gifts. I completed Tina's OBM training and became one of the very first Certified OBMs. I had the honor of working with Tina as her OBM for many years, which allowed me to not only do my best work but to provide support to a community of OBMs who are changing the way businesses are run. In 2015 I

started a digital agency with my husband, where I have taken everything I learned as an OBM and poured it into a business that currently has 5 full-time employees and services between 15 and 20 clients a month. To say that the OBM book changed my life would be an understatement. If you read this book and find yourself in its pages just know that you are about to begin the adventure of a lifetime."
Tiffany Johnson, Certified OBM

"Tina Forsyth's book *Becoming an Online Business Manager'* quite literally changed my life. When I picked up Tina's book I had just quit my job and had no idea what was next. As soon as I started reading I knew I had found my next career. Tina's book led me down a path that has allowed me to create a life I didn't even know was possible. I now do the work I love to do, live the life I want to live, and make great money doing it... and it all started with Tina's book. Entering Tina's world was one of the best decisions I ever made, and I will be forever grateful for her and her powerful book."
Dori Tattrie, Certified OBM

"Before becoming an OBM, I was struggling to find my way in the industry. I had a single client that I was working for full-time as a Techie VA while I learned the industry, watched the big players and noticed I had this gut feeling like there was something more for me. I'd spent years as a Project Manager and corporate employee but couldn't seem to find where I fit into the entrepreneur world. Then I found Tina's book *Becoming an Online Business Manager* - I couldn't put it down and read the entire thing in a couple days! Throughout the whole book I kept thinking "This is me, this is what I do right now!" and I knew that I WAS an Online Business Manager. I became a Certified OBM in 2015 and am now the COO of a successful 7-figure business, managing a team of 14 people and working closely with my client to grow the business. More importantly, I'm home every day with my family, I attend my kids' activities and school events, and I feel like my business has been built around my life instead of the other way around!"

Jenn Sebastian, Certified OBM

"Returning to the workforce after 10 years at home to raise my kids was a very daunting prospect. I felt my resume was disjointed. I'd worked across 11 different industries and had just as many role descriptions – there was no clear career path let alone industry loyalty. Add to that I still want to be around for my kids outside of school hours. Who was I and what would I do? Then I read *Becoming an Online Business Manager*. Wowsers! All roads did lead somewhere after all.

Every part of the book made sense. It was an easy read and very clearly expressed the opportunities and foundation in how to perform as an OBM. My diverse experience all came together perfectly. I launched my business and paid for the OBM Certification Training with my very first client. Now I know I'm serving my clients how they need it while honoring their business. Now I have a career that I love, is challenging me in all the right ways, supports my family and allows me to be home for my kids."
Melissa Pritchard, Certified OBM

"Since becoming a Certified OBM I have to turn away prospects because I have a full practice. My clients are always referring me to their tribe - word of mouth has become my greatest marketing tool. I am now able to easily reach my monthly income goals and then some :) I no longer feel unfulfilled like I did when I was working as a VA and like there is more I can be doing to help my clients grow. Being an Online Business Manager allows me to be involved in every aspect of my client's business. My clients' success is my success and that is the most "rewarding" feeling. I am living the life and it is all thanks to Tina and her Online Business Manager Training. I couldn't be happier in my business. So, if you are on the fence about becoming an OBM, my recommendation is to "just do it", believe in yourself and make it happen!"
Josie Martinez, Certified OBM

"After a long military career, I found myself uncertain as to what was next. Shortly after my son was born I was forced to go back to work too early and ended up getting a civilian Federal job as an Office Administrator. Leaving my son to go to work was the hardest thing I had to do. Not only were my commutes sucking the life out of me, my duties kept increasing and I wasn't getting paid more for it. I knew I couldn't keep working this way. I explored becoming a virtual assistant but I knew that wasn't it - after all my years of experience and leadership in the military, it felt like a demotion. Then I read Tina's *Becoming an Online Business Manager* book and it was as if she was speaking right to me. Since reading the book and becoming a Certified OBM the changes in my own business have been amazing. I have gotten focused, been more productive and created a better brand for my business. I have been able to find clients that fit, who I want to work with and I am making more money. All those things are great, but what I'm most grateful for is the service and support I received during times of uncertainty. Now that I know my path all things are possible."

Jules Sanchez, Certified OBM

"Before becoming a Certified OBM I was working at a low-level management job. I had no flexibility, no ability to delegate and I had really no way to make more money.

All my efforts to do my job well got was verbal praise - but my life never improved. It was after the birth of my second baby, who ended up being sick and hospitalized, that I realized I did NOT want to go back to corporate America. I felt like being a mother and wanting flexibility made me less of an employee - but I did not know what else was available! It was another mom friend who introduced me to the VA world. I thrived as a VA - but after a few years I knew I could do more - I could manage, not just do. Then I read Tina's book and I knew - I was meant to become an OBM. Since taking the training and becoming Certified in 2016 I've more than tripled my income. (15K to 65K) and am working better hours. I have weekends off and take 2 vacations every year. My clients have brought in a team and now I manage them, and I know how to effectively delegate to the team. I am SO much happier. I feel like I finally found my tribe and when things get heated and hard - I know who to turn to. My advice for those thinking of becoming an OBM is that it's ok to be scared. Being an OBM is a huge step - but you are NOT alone and if your gut says "maybe I can do it" - follow that. I am so thankful I took a leap. Being an OBM feels so natural to me and I am thankful to have Tina and her team to turn to."
Martha Gerber, Certified OBM

"Before becoming an OBM I was a virtual assistant for about 2 1/2 years and it just wasn't lighting me up anymore. I wanted to work less and make more money in a way that would have been impossible as a VA. Plus I was tired with the mundane doing and wanted to step into a more systems-oriented, strategic role for my clients. Thanks to Tina's book and the OBM certification course I can now charge my worth, work only with people I want to work with, fill a bigger role in my client's companies, AND work fewer hours with a bigger paycheck. Working with Tina has been a total game changer because she gets it and all her advice is specifically targeted to this industry (unlike the many generic business trainers out there.) The biggest change has come from my ability to own what I do and to define it in a way that makes sense to people who've never heard of an OBM before. I now feel confident in what I offer clients."

Meaghan Lamm, Certified OBM

"I started my VA business 8 years ago after being downsized - I realized that I did not want to work hard as an employee anymore where my only ROI was just a paycheck. Soon after I started working as a VA, I realized that I was more than a VA but I didn't know what to call myself! Nor did I know how to explain it to others. After I read Tina's book I knew I had found it - *Becoming an Online Business Manager* expressed & articulated what I do. Since becoming a Certified OBM I have started a VA agency and am providing OBM level services to my clients. I am continuing to transition from being the doer (this is harder than you think) to being the leader. Of course, my revenue has increased but I have also added 2 amazing women to my team and am now able to pay it forward and invest in their lives just as Tina and her team have invested in mine.

My advice is as follows: If this book is speaking your language...then this is the tribe for you. Get off the sidelines and make the investment in yourself and your business. You can choose to do it by yourself, but it will take longer, and you will make mistakes that you could possibly avoid if you are connected to this community. The ROI will depend on your commitment to the process and transformation, but it will be well worth it and not just monetarily, but in other priceless intangible ways."
Erica Bell, Certified OBM

"Before becoming a Certified OBM I built two service-based companies online that gave me an income, but I was always frustrated with the "feast or famine" ride of the online entrepreneurial world. I tried and tried to solve this issue on my own to no avail. Also, no one understood what

I did, and I had a hard time telling them, so sales were hard. When I became an OBM this all changed. I am now able to talk with confidence about what I do and sell my services at a level I've never known before. I gained the skills and expertise I needed to catapult me to a new level through the Certified OBM program. The thing I loved the most about the training was that Tina and her team know the journey of becoming an Online Business Manager as they have been on this road themselves. They understand it in and out. Their advice, leadership, and willingness to 'be real' made this program challenging but rewarding. I will always believe this was one of the best things I have done for my business."

Paula Allen, Certified OBM

"Before becoming an OBM I felt that there was something missing. I started my business as a VA and felt like I was so much more - I just didn't know exactly what! I seemed to be quite good at everything and was the ideal right-hand woman for business owners, but I didn't have a specialty, so I found it hard to charge what I thought I was worth. And I was also frustrated by having to charge by the hour and knew I wouldn't be able to scale my business that way. As a Certified OBM, I have the qualifications to back up my experience and I can now confidently charge what I am worth with no hesitation. I am currently in Cyprus on holiday with my family for 2 weeks where I am not needed to step into the day to day running of the business. WOW! It's an amazing feeling to have a business that works around our crazy life."

Kelly-Marie West, Certified OBM

"I have a varied background. I am a professional engineer by education as well as a trained massage therapist. In my career, I have contributed to global warming research around the globe, assisted in editing scientific journals and worked with narcotics detection instrumentation. But, it was when I started working in office management for a small engineering company that things started to make sense to me - I knew then that I wanted to work with small businesses going forward. I had found my tribe! For personal reasons I left this company and did contract work with two separate virtual companies. This opened my mind to the possibility of working virtually AND with small business. However, in starting my own business, I found it challenging to find clients through traditional means. I didn't know how to describe what I was doing in a way that made sense to my potential clients, or to myself! When I discovered the OBM community I knew I had found my home. I am more confident in speaking to prospects since I know and understand their businesses from their perspective and thus I am able to sell myself better. The community is a goldmine of amazing people that will support you in whatever you choose to do. If you can find the determination to do this, you will make it with their help!"

Erika Biesenthal, Certified OBM

"In my previous career I worked as a corporate marketing director for accountants and had a side hustle as a VA. I'm what they call an accidental OBM... I was hanging out, just fine in corporate not realizing that the work I was doing was so much more. In the side hustle as a VA, I never really realized I was performing stuff that really wasn't just VA work. I just thought "everyone does this" and kept moving. Once I was laid off from my corporate gig, I sought out more VA opportunities as I looked for a new job. I was working with a small team of people in 2010, when the owner of the biz went to an event and one of the sessions was Tina speaking on OBM's and why you need one. She entered the session thinking, "I don't have a need for this - my biz is too little." She exited the session thinking, "I need an OBM now and I think I know who it is. She's already on my team!" (it was me). After a call with Tina I knew - not only was I meant to be an OBM I was already doing it! And

it was time to make it official, which I did in 2011 and I haven't looked back."
Ericka Pardun, Certified OBM

"Before reading this book I remember feeling confused about what to call myself. I was doing VA work, yes, but I was also doing work that I knew was way beyond the scope of a VA. I decided to just go with "VA" because it seemed like the easiest way to share with others what I do. As time went by I felt resentment creeping up on me because of two main things: 1.) I realized calling myself a VA was a disservice to my clients and myself. 2.) The work was beginning to feel monotonous. I wanted to be more involved in my clients' business. I wanted to be proactive in helping my clients to grow their business. So I started to call myself an OBM but oh boy did I feel consumed by an avalanche of doubt! Am I doing it right? What don't I know? Am I charging too low/too high? With the training & support I received, my confidence is shooting through the roof! I now know exactly what to do and how to do the things that would help grow my clients' business. My advice for those thinking of becoming an OBM is read Tina's book, *Becoming an Online Business Manager*. Read it at least twice. Get a feel for what's possible. And then if you feel a yes, GO FOR IT!"
Mona Rose Moore, Certified OBM

"I have been a Freelancer since 2003 and an Agency Owner since 2009. What I didn't realize was that I was actually working as an OBM for my clients! It just came naturally to me. When I discovered this becoming an Online Business Manager and making it official was the obvious next step, and I'm proud to be the first ever "Certified OBM in the Philippines" by the IAOBM. My advice for those thinking of becoming an OBM is - don't think twice! Becoming an OBM is not as easy as it sounds, like what Uncle Ben said to Peter "With great power comes great responsibility". It may sound hard but imagine the value that you will be able to give to your clients and how you will be able to help them achieve their business goals. As a result, there will be great opportunities that will come knocking on your door and you will not need to look for clients. They will come looking for you."

Allie Pasag, Certified OBM

10th Anniversary Edition

BECOMING AN ONLINE BUSINESS MANAGER

By Tina Forsyth

with contributions from Sharon Broughton,
Keldie Jamieson, and Sarah Noked

Love Your Life

Becoming an Online Business Manager-10th Anniversary Edition

Love Your Life Publishing

427 N Tatnall St.

Wilmington, DE 19801

ISBN: 978-1-934509-94-4

Author Contact:

Tina Forsyth

(403) 830-4339

tina@tinaforsyth.com

Editor: Linda Dessau, www.LindaDessau.com

Book Cover Design: Sarah Barrie, www.Cyanotype.ca

Book Layout Design: Balaji Selvadurai

TABLE OF CONTENTS

FOREWORD

Dear Online Business Manager (and business owner too), I have hired and fired more than my fair share of Virtual Assistants. Sometimes, it was my fault they didn't work out, but nine times out of ten it was because they didn't have the tools to be worth the investment. They didn't have the skills that are taught in this book. They didn't have the resources that are detailed in this book. And, they didn't have the knowledge that can be gleaned from this book.

As a Virtual Assistant or Online Business Manager, what do you do for the business owners who hire you? Sure, you make their life easier, but there's so much more you could be doing. You have the power to help them make more money while reducing their costs.

Most VAs and other online support professionals come **from** an administrative background and have a preconceived notion that their role is to take on the things that the business owner either a) doesn't like doing or b) doesn't know how to do. Their focus is on freeing up the business owner to have more time and a better lifestyle.

But if you want to earn an invaluable place in your client's business, not to mention higher and higher fees, that's not enough.

The key is to change your mindset from how can I make this business owner's life easier to **how can I help grow this business?**

For some, this requires a subtle shift in thinking. For others, the shift is revolutionary. Either way, its impact can speak volumes. And I can tell you that as a business owner, this kind of support is extremely hard to find. I talk to business owners every day who are not getting the kind of support that they need, and it almost always comes down to mindset — their VAs are thinking *administratively* instead of *strategically*. They are great people with excellent skills but their focus rests too narrowly on details and not enough on the big picture.

Having finally learned the secret to healthy, prosperous and meaningful relationships with my team, I no longer hire someone who can simply "help me out." I will only hire people and teams who understand my business and are truly invested in the success and growth of what we are creating. I need to be able to see the ROI from my team members, to measure what they have to offer for my investment. And they need to be able to tell me specifically how they will do this. If they can't demonstrate their value to my business (not just to me) I won't work with them.

Why would they do this — invest so heavily in my success? Because my success is their success. As I make more money, they make more money. As I learn more, they learn more. As I do bigger and bigger things, they do bigger and bigger things. And the reverse is also true. As they learn more, I learn more. As they do bigger and bigger things, I do bigger and bigger things.

As business owners and online support professionals, together we can do more than we can do alone, but only if you make the shift from Virtual Assistant to Online Business Manager.

This book will show you how to make that shift. You'll learn the actual "how to" specifics of the Online Business Manager role and you'll also learn about the crucial mindset that you'll need; because ultimately, it's the way you think that will determine your future.

Face it – there is virtually no room for growth or promotion as a VA. You may be able to slightly increase your rates, year-by-year, but that will only get you so far. The OBM, on the other hand, has exponential room for growth — even if you start small you can work to add more value to the business (e.g., managing, planning or leading) and grow into more senior positions over time. This also gives you the opportunity to tie your compensation into the revenues and/or profits of the business which can blow the roof off of what you can make from an hourly wage. The more you help grow your client's business the more you earn as well — everyone wins!

A quick shout out to my fellow small business owners: Why should you read this book? It will give you a priceless and essential understanding of what an OBM can do for you. After all, what's the point of owning your own business? I believe it's to live a better, more fulfilling and financially independent life. And an OBM can help you achieve that. This book will give you insight into how to find, hire and manage your OBM, what expectations to set for them and how to get the best work out of them. If you want to do big things in the world, plan on hiring an OBM and keep on reading to discover how.

And finally, why is Tina Forsyth the one to write this book? Simply put, she is the best of class. She was serving as an OBM before anyone had ever heard of such a thing. She has been training and certifying Online Business Managers now for 10 years. And, most importantly, she has the utmost integrity. She does what she says she's going to do, and then some.

I hope that your professional path is filled with abundance, meaning and joy and that your dreams are realized through an expression of your faith, inner-strength and confidence.

Think big,

Michael Port, *NY Times, WSJ* bestselling author of 7 books including *Steal the Show* and *Book Yourself Solid*.

INTRODUCTION

I remember graduating from college with my business degree in 1994 and talking with my classmates about our careers. What we wanted to do for a living, our big dreams and goals.

I never could have imagined then what I was really going to be doing when I "grew up": working from home as an online-based business owner. The Internet barely even existed in 1994 – I don't think I even had my first email address until a couple years later!

It is an awesome world that we live in, where people and business can be connected beyond the "brick and mortar" of the traditional working environment. I've worked online since 1999, first as an "online community manager" with a start-up magazine for twenty-somethings (boy, were we ahead of our time there - think social networking before there was a term for it) next as an Online Business Manager (OBM) for multiple 6 & 7-figure online businesses and since 2009 as a trainer and mentor of hundreds of Certified Online Business Managers.

And if one thing is constant in this type of work, it is the fact that there is a HUGE demand for virtual business support, whether the business itself is based online or it's a regular offline business just looking for someone to manage their online presence. The demand has been growing steadily for 10 years now and we have now reached a 'critical mass' where OBMs are now considered an essential part of a business team. As online business owners continue to grow their own ventures they reach the point where they need to hire at the management level. They already have teams of virtual assistants, social media and marketing professionals, webmasters, designers and other contractors, but what they really need is someone to manage all of this; to *play a bigger role* in their business so that they can grow to the next level.

I believe that there are many professionals out there who have the skills to be working as an OBM; they just haven't realized that this opportunity exists. Having worked virtually for almost two decades now, it's easy for me to forget that this way of working is still new to most people. And because of that there is a gap between the business owners who are looking to hire OBMs and the people who could potentially be working for them in his role.

Why is there such an alarming gap?

For business owners, it is a matter of not knowing who or what they are really looking for. They may have a faint idea they could benefit from hiring someone to help them manage and grow their business online, but they often have no clue what that role looks like. They aren't clear themselves on what it is they need, which of course makes it quite hard to find someone! Quite often, when we describe the role of an OBM to the business owners we speak to, we hear, "Yes! THAT's exactly who I need on my team ... now where do I find someone?"

That's why I'm writing this book ...

I want to connect those who want to hire an OBM with someone like you - a (soon to be) professional Certified OBM®.

Many people – whether they are actively working online or not – have the aptitude and skill set to be able to play this bigger role with clients, they just don't know that the opportunity is out there. Is this starting to sound a little like you, perhaps? Whether you're a new graduate from business school, an experienced former corporate manager, or just someone with the gumption to try it, I hope you're ready to consider a world of immense possibility that opens up opportunities you may have only dreamed of. It's kinda like me planning my career back in '94. I had no clue that the option to work this way with clients was even a possibility. Not so many years later, here I am, doing what was once considered impossible.

My mission in writing this book is simple – it's to help you, the future Online Business Manager, open your eyes to the possibility of doing this for a living. And yes, it can be a very lucrative living.

As you read this book, if you find yourself saying, "YES! This is me, I totally want to do this– bring it on!" then I will have achieved what I set out to do here. To allow you a space to recognize and hopefully start to move towards playing this bigger role with new and existing clients.

I invite you to learn more about how to become a Certified OBM® at www.certifiedobm.com.

CHAPTER 1

TO BE OR NOT TO BE - HOW DO I KNOW IF I'M A POTENTIAL OBM?

"Blaze a path of your own brilliance"

Becoming an OBM is a great choice for anyone who wants professional challenge, stimulating and enjoyable clients and a freedom-based lifestyle. If your spidey senses are already telling you that you're an OBM, feel free to jump ahead to the next chapter. Otherwise, read through this chapter and be sure to spend a few minutes to take the 'Am I Ready to Become an OBM' Assessment at the end.

There are three types of professionals who are especially well suited to this type of work. This isn't an exclusive list by any means – anyone with a marketing mindset and an interest in online business can certainly work towards becoming an OBM. However, after 10 years of training

OBMs I consider these folks to be 'on the cusp' of playing this bigger role. What they do already is so close to the role of an OBM, that a simple shift in what they offer could very quickly have them working at this level with paying clients.

1. Virtual Assistants at the bursting point in their businesses

Virtual Assistants (VAs), those unseen angels who do a variety of tasks for their clients from a home-based office, are struggling; not so much from a lack of business as from an over-abundance of business.

Yes, just like in any profession, there are new VAs out there who are just getting started and are struggling to find clients and get their business off the ground. However, many VAs are reaching a critical point in their businesses - having **too much** business coming their way - which in itself brings a whole new set of challenges.

When I launched an online recruitment and matching service for VAs back in 2005, I worked with hundreds of VAs and saw a common path in the growth of their businesses:

- VA starts a new business
- VA gets a few clients and some good experience under their belt

- VA's clients refer them to other potential clients (of which there are always plenty!)
- VA says yes to these new clients and soon has a full business
- VA's business becomes "uncomfortably full". They are getting so much work from various clients that it is hard to keep up (and life becomes super stressful)

This is what I call the **bursting point.** If you're a VA who's even remotely capable, and you haven't experienced the bursting point yet, trust me, you will. Any VA who has the hot skills that clients are looking for will very soon be full-to-bursting with clients.

It's like eating a huge meal at Thanksgiving; you are so full you could burst, but the food is so good you just can't say no!

The bursting point is your rite of passage

The bursting point isn't necessarily a bad thing, right? You have what you wanted from your VA business, which was to be busy and make some good money. I consider the bursting point to be a rite of passage in a Virtual Assistant's business; we all need to go through it in order to define what we do best and who we want to work with.

The thing is, though, that living in the bursting point is not sustainable in the long run. The bursting point is like a bubble, and if you stay in it too long, it is a guarantee that you will see the effects of imbalance in your life and that bubble will eventually pop with a messy splat, negative side effects touching everyone within range.

Signs that you are at the bursting point:

- You don't have enough hours in the day to get your work done, and you are falling behind on many of your commitments
- You are feeling overwhelmed and are starting to dread hearing from your clients
- Clients are starting to get upset with you as the work is coming late, is not complete or is incorrect
- Your family and friends are asking you, "Why do you work so much?" or "Are you on that computer again?"
- You don't have time to say yes to any new and exciting projects or clients that come your way (including those that pay a higher rate)
- Work has become a drag; you aren't enjoying it anymore and may even start to avoid it or get depressed (this is a big sign of burnout!)

Does any of this sound familiar to you? If yes, you may very well be at the bursting point in your business.

The cure for some is as simple as saying, "No more clients, I'm full," or even cutting back on your current client load to get back to a more sane and stable pace.

But what if you want to continue to grow your business? What if you are busy but you're still not making the kind of money you want to make? Or what if you would like to work less but continue to make a good wage?

You may be ready to graduate to working as an Online Business Manager for your clients.

2. An Online Business Manager in disguise ...

There are many online professionals who are already doing OBM level work for their clients but don't realize it, and because of that are selling themselves short in the marketplace and even in the eyes of their current clients.

OBMs in disguise usually come to realize that they are doing more than what the virtual assistant or online support role calls for. It's like the administrative assistant who's really acting as HR Manager. Or the Executive Assistant who's slowly taken on duties of the former Operations Director, only hasn't received the title or pay raise. High time to make an adjustment, wouldn't you say?

There comes a point when they realize that they are "doing more." In some instances, in fact, it's their client who points this out:

Sharon Broughton was about 5 years into her VA career and had gained a ton of knowledge and expertise about online marketing, launches, newsletters, websites,

Infusionsoft, and more. She had been working with a client for a few years as a VA. Her responsibilities had morphed over time into being more and more involved in the day to day of the business, managing projects and the team.

One day her client asked her if she knew she was acting as an OBM. Sharon hadn't realized it because she was just doing what needed to be done. The client was thrilled she was getting the extra attention for her business and told Sharon that she was doing it beautifully. Until her client pointed it out to her, Sharon didn't realize she was doing anything out of the ordinary, she was just doing what came naturally to her. She became a Certified OBM® in 2010 and has been serving clients at this level ever since.

Or the OBM-in-disguise may one day compare what they are doing to what their colleagues are doing.

As a VA, Amy naturally "took charge" of projects for her clients, sharing her ideas, brainstorming and always looking for ways to work better with them. When she looked around at other VAs, she noticed that she went beyond the simple "task assistance" they were providing, and instead was successfully contributing to her clients' projects from concept right through to completion. In playing this bigger role, Amy felt more competent, because she began to see her clients businesses as a "whole" and not just as a sum of the tasks she performed. Her clients began to love this management role that she was taking on, as it freed up their time even further. Again, this is just what came naturally to her. When she noticed this, Amy shifted how she presented herself and her services. She called herself an OBM and priced her services accordingly.

There are a lot of folks out there who are already providing OBM-level support, but haven't formalized that role, and as such, aren't being compensated properly.

In the next section we will be diving into the role of the OBM, and what exactly they do for their clients. If you find yourself saying, "Hey, that's what I already do!" then you may be an OBM in disguise. You've probably always known that you are "doing a bit more," but haven't really been able to articulate it to yourself or your clients. If that is the case, this book will give you the clarity to officially take on this role and enjoy the satisfaction and compensation that come alongside.

3. Business-savvy professionals who are ready to start serving online based businesses

I once met a woman who had been running a very successful embroidery business with her husband, where he was the tech whiz and she was the marketing pro. After selling the business, she decided she wanted to work online. Not necessarily as a VA, but to help clients use the power of the Internet to grow their businesses.

"Sounds like you want to be an Online Business Manager," I said to her. After explaining to her a bit more of what the role is about, she was thrilled to realize that it was even a possibility!

Being a successful business owner herself, she already has what I call a marketing mindset (I'll speak more about this in the next section), which is an essential piece of being a successful OBM.

Keldie Jamieson has a similar story that some of you may relate to:

> In 2009 the business I was working at closed and I knew I didn't want to get another corporate "job". I didn't want to depend on anyone else to keep the money flowing anymore. I was tired of the lay-offs and office politics that I had been dealing with for 25 years and wanted to be home and "available" to my kids now that they were teens. I had been researching the online world for about 4 years already and was thinking that becoming a virtual assistant was my best option. But I didn't really want to go back to being just an assistant or to become a tech freelancer. I wanted to help online business owners run

their business like I did in the corporate world but wasn't sure what to call myself.

Then I one day I found Tina online, read her book Becoming an Online Business Manager and everything just fell into place. I was an online business manager! Even though I knew this was my path I still wasn't confident I could transition my corporate expertise into a profitable online career and business, so I signed up for her Certified OBM® Training. Doing the training gave me the skills I was missing and skyrocketed my confidence. I became a Certified OBM in 2011 and have had a profitable and successful business ever since.

With a strong business background and marketing mindset, anyone can learn the online tools and skills necessary to become an OBM.

After all, business is business. Whether it is an online or traditional business it all boils down to the same thing - create value that people will pay for.

This type of potential OBM is probably one of the most exciting to me, especially when I consider someone like the stay-at-home mom or dad. They have chosen to stay home with their children instead of going back to work and may have amazing business and marketing skills that are lying dormant.

Many of them would love to be able to work, if only there was an opportunity that allowed them the flexibility to be home with their children while making a living. I know there are potential OBMs at home watching (yet another!) episode of Barney and wishing they could use their brain for more than memorizing the songs from kid shows.

Or, as anyone who has ever worked in the corporate world knows, there are MANY talented people out there who are under-utilized and essentially miserable in their jobs. (This could be you!)

It is to these business-savvy professionals in particular that I send a "virtual poke" to consider becoming an Online Business Manager.

Online Business Manager Aptitude and Attitude Assessment

Curious if you are ready to become an OBM? Take the assessment below and find out where you land.

>> You can also take this assessment online at www.obmquiz.com <<

Score yourself on a scale of 1-5 for each of the statements below, with 1 being, "No way, that's not me at all!" and 5 being, "Oh, yeah, it's like looking in a mirror!"

I thrive on the challenge of being thrown into new (and sometimes) uncertain situations.	1	2	3	4	5
I am inspired by a big vision, and automatically start thinking of what it will take to bring that big vision to life (the steps, resources, etc.)	1	2	3	4	5
I am self-motivated and don't need someone to tell me what to do to get the job done.	1	2	3	4	5
I am proactive and prefer to create a plan for everyone to work from vs. perpetually flying by the seat of our pants.	1	2	3	4	5
I am driven to 'get things done' and love nothing more than checking something off the to-do list and seeing a project come to completion!	1	2	3	4	5
I connect easily with people online and enjoy communicating via telephone, email and instant message.	1	2	3	4	5
I enjoy and understand the value of working with a team and get satisfaction from seeing my contribution to the bigger picture.	1	2	3	4	5
I am motivated by helping others to do great work and giving them the tools and resources they need to accomplish their tasks.	1	2	3	4	5

I am comfortable taking responsibility for the overall success of the team and not just for my own tasks.	1	2	3	4	5
I am not easily intimidated by 'big' personalities and love the energy of the creatively driven business owner.	1	2	3	4	5
I have a general understanding and love of "all things business."	1	2	3	4	5
I am always looking for the best way to accomplish a task and get frustrated when things are overly complicated or messy.	1	2	3	4	5
I stay calm in the middle of confusion and chaos and will naturally take charge to fix a situation when issues arise.	1	2	3	4	5
I understand the importance of having clearly designed processes that allow the team to get the right work done in the right way.	1	2	3	4	5
I don't mind rolling my sleeves up and getting my hands dirty "doing the work" when required.	1	2	3	4	5
I am familiar with and/or have hands-on experience in online marketing.	1	2	3	4	5
I can easily learn "on the fly" and am not afraid to figure things out as I go.	1	2	3	4	5

I am tech savvy and understand the systems required to run a successful online business.	I	2	3	4	5
I don't take things personally and know that there is always room for improvement and growth.	I	2	3	4	5
I have a suitable home office environment, free of distractions and with all the tools I need to work efficiently.	I	2	3	4	5

If you scored 1–40

You're not quite there yet. This is a great time to open yourself up to new learning, experiences and opportunities, with the possibility of becoming an Online Business Manager in the future. Read on to learn more about this role and see if this is something you may want to work towards.

If you scored 41-70

You have a strong aptitude and foundation for the OBM role and are ready to hone your skills to take it up to the next level. We recommend continuing to expand your OBM skillset and to explore your training options to get you ready to work at this level.

If you scored 71–100

It sounds like you are well on your way to becoming – or may already be working as - an Online Business Manager.

Woo hoo! Use the following chapters to clarify what it is you have to offer, what you want to accomplish for your clients (and yourself) and to fill in any remaining gaps in your skillset.

Learn more about your training options and next steps at www.CertifiedOBM.com

CHAPTER 2

GIVE THEM WHAT THEY WANT - WHAT CLIENTS ARE ASKING FOR

The Role of the Online Business Manager

I like to look at the role of the Online Business Manager through the lens of *how we help support our clients.*

What do clients need? What are they asking for help with (and having trouble finding!)? What is truly going to help them grow and expand their business?

After all, if it wasn't for the needs of our clients, the role of the Online Business Manager wouldn't mean anything. We are here to serve them and their businesses, so it is essential to really understand their needs to provide the best level of support.

I've spoken to thousands of small business owners over the past 10 years who are desperately seeking the help of an Online Business Manager. They didn't know that's what they needed; they just knew they needed help!

Here are some of the most common challenges that people have shared with us:

- "I am so overwhelmed and just can't do this on my own anymore – help!"

- "I'm making a good living, but just can't seem to make my business grow beyond where I am now."

- "I've worked with a bunch of VAs but I can't seem to find one that can do what I need. Why is it so hard to find the right person?"

- "There's so much going on in my business but I'm not sure what is getting done and what isn't. I wish I had someone to manage all those pieces for me."

- "My brain is bursting with new ideas for my business, but I'm busy enough as it is. I guess all these ideas will have to wait ..."

When the client is ready ...

In general, clients are ready (and asking!) to hire an OBM when they realize that they can't do it all themselves anymore. Key phrase in that sentence – THEY need to realize it. You may see a client who is struggling with their business because they can't do it all on their own, but if they don't see that and aren't willing to change it then hiring an OBM won't do them a lick of good.

The role of the OBM boils down to one simple thing:

You are freeing up your client so that they can focus their time and energy on the things that only THEY can do to grow their business.

A question that we recommend all our clients to ask themselves throughout their work day is:

Is this something only I can do?

If the answer is yes (usually things like setting their vision, marketing, product development and forming and nurturing strategic alliances), we tell them to keep on doing it. If the answer is no, we suggest that it's time for them to let go of that task and pass it on to their team. For many business owners this can be a very tough yet liberating journey. They are used to doing everything on their own, and it takes some time to break the habits of doing the things that really aren't the best use of their time.

And in some cases, the client may even be hiding behind some of these tasks so that they don't have to go out and do the business-building tasks required of them. A client of ours made a point of hiring a bookkeeper for her business, not because she disliked the task but because she enjoyed it! Instead of doing her business-building activities she would distract herself with bookkeeping, and so she hired someone to take it off her plate and take away her distraction. Very smart.

These distractions are what you can take care of as the OBM. You're not stepping in to do all the work; your role is to manage all the pieces so that the business owner can be free to focus on growth and expansion.

Here is an example of an actual Online Business Manager opportunity that was originally posted (and filled) within our Certified OBM® community.

LOOKING FOR A ROCKSTAR ONLINE BUSINESS MANAGER

We are looking to fill this important role on our team to ensure that "stuff gets done" on time and to high standards. As the OBM you are responsible for managing all projects (including activities of the team) to full delivery of all milestones. You take pride in seeing projects through to completion, on time, accurately and in keeping with the company's standards of quality and client care. The ultimate goal is to have a solid right-hand person who will fully own the operations side of the business.

The Online Business manager is expected to help meet our deadlines and function as a backup to other team members where required. In the first several months, there will be the expectation of some 'doing' along with 'managing' in order to learn the business to setup and identify solid systems, and also to "fill the gap" until additional team members are hired. The intention is to hire other team members as mutually determined by the OBM and the business owner after an analysis of business needs in the first 90-days.

The Ideal Person for this role:

- Has at least 2 years of applicable on-line experience in one or more of the fields of marketing, ecommerce, coaching, project management, personal development or other related area of study

- Wants to OWN the business management side of the business. Has a love of taking charge and full ownership of operations as well as projects; bringing them from idea to completion. You love to see a project or task completed and will do whatever it takes to get the job done, including doing the work yourself!

- Can thrive and deliver while working on SHORT timeframes in a fast-paced environment; juggling multiple projects simultaneously

- Is results oriented; you are a self starter, an independent thinker with an income producing mindset

- Can easily handle multiple tasks, projects and vendors, juggle multiple tasks simultaneously, manage and prioritize minute-by-minute and is exceptionally responsive

- Can thrive working independently, from home, on the road or on-site (if required.)

- Has a love of internet marketing, direct response marketing, and personal development and a familiarity / practical experience in the execution of all facets of online business, including launches, copywriting, product planning and creation, traffic generation.

- Pride in always bringing your "A" game. Confident in yourself and your skill set.

- A superstar attitude with a warm and embracing personality. Truly believes in and is in alignment with the spirituality of the business

- High value for strategic planning, organization and execution, plus an obsessive eye for detail and proofing

- An active, open, honest communicator, loves being part of a team, loves contributing to others

- Can offer a strong commitment to the business owner, coming in with the mindset of a partner and protect their time and energy (plus carry the vision for the business and have a strong desire to be a part of it)

- Understands affiliate programs and joint ventures; can hold and cultivate key relationships.

- A strong marketing mindset with the understanding of how your role and all decisions need to contribute to serving clients and the overall growth of the business.

- Experience with project management software and the ability to create and run the full implementation of a project via online software.

- A working knowledge of Infusionsoft, with the ability to send broadcasts and act as technical backup.

- Offer a brilliantly positive attitude and bring solutions to the table when a challenge is faced

Specific Responsibilities:

- Manage multiple (and concurrent) projects from idea to execution, including the creation of a project plan and implementation of an online, centralized project management system.

- Develop and maintain a standard operating procedure and business training manual for the business – all systems and procedures will need to be recorded and managed.

- Manage the technology and details of our training programs, including scheduling classes, sending reminders, managing recordings/materials and implementation of a training resource center for all programs.

- Identification of and sourcing of team members as required, for projects or on and on-going basis. (i.e.: Hiring a techie VA)

- Delegate to various members of the team (including vendors) for completion of applicable tasks, setting priorities and ongoing follow-up as required.

- Implementation (doing) of applicable tasks within projects with an eye for detail and the ability to dive into the "nitty gritty" aspects of what needs to be done.

- Communicate with joint venture and affiliate partners, managing details of marketing calendar, promotional copy and keeping partners happy.

- Review website and information product content for improvement and accuracy.
- Collaborate on creation of new products or programs — working with the team to setup systems and structure for any new offerings.
- Create and maintain detailed launch calendars for online promotions.

Commitment: This is a virtually based position that requires you to have the equipment and capability to work from your own home office. Most of the work will be performed virtually, though the willingness to travel to our events may be required. We are in the Pacific Time zone and while you are not expected to conduct all work during this period, you must be available as required during regular working hours in this time zone. Critical business items, updates and reports must be provided during working business hours.

A commitment of 30-40 hours a month to start is required, with the availability to grow into a more dedicated role as the business reaches various milestones. Work on evenings and weekends may be required from time to time during launches or events but is not expected as standard.

Is that a position you would have loved to fill? Great! You'll have a chance to fill that same kind of role for your own clients as an OBM.

Now that you have a general sense of what the Online Business Manager role is, let's go ahead and dive deeper into the specifics.

CHAPTER 3

IT ALL STARTS HERE – THE MARKETING MINDSET

Clients want someone to brainstorm with,
be proactive and make decisions

Clients are looking for someone who will treat their business as if it were their own. They realize they can't be everywhere or do everything, so they want the next best thing.

And that's why having a marketing mindset is the foundation of working as an Online Business Manager. It's the one essential skill that is not negotiable.

A colleague recently shared a story with me that I think illustrates this beautifully. A couple of years ago, one of her clients moved out of the country. When they got to their new destination they were unable to get an Internet connection for almost four months, which meant that her client had NO way to log in and manage their already successful online business. She stepped in and took over the reins, making sure that her client's business continued to run while they were unavailable. When her client was able to finally get online, everything was still running smoothly, and their business continues to grow to this day.

In her own words she said "I treat my client's business as my own – I care whether or not there is a sale that day, whether or not customers are happy. I don't just 'do the tasks' assigned to me, I'm always considering the big picture of their business and how I can help in ways that are beyond what is asked of me."

This is the heart of what the marketing mindset is all about. When working for your clients as OBM, you are truly invested in the growth and success of their business. You look at all aspects of your client's business as though it were your own business.

It's just like someone who is looking for a good daycare provider for their children. They want someone who will treat their children with love and respect and will also provide an environment in which they can grow and thrive. For clients, their business is their child and a good OBM provides the same loving care.

Know your stuff

The marketing mindset starts with having a **strong understanding of the client's business model.**

You really need to understand how your client makes money. How does their industry work? What are they selling? What is path of their sales funnel from prospect to customer? Who is their target market and what are they doing to reach them?

This comes down to literally being able to *speak the same language* as your client.

While working with my friend Andrea Lee back in 2004, we were constantly approached by clients looking to hire virtual assistants (VAs) and other online support professionals. We quickly started to see a common challenge that many business owners were facing – they were hiring VAs but it wasn't working out.

This was usually for one very simple reason: the virtual assistant didn't understand what the client was trying to accomplish in their business. They didn't get the "big picture," and as such they had a really hard time providing a thorough level of support for the client's needs. The client would say, "I need to create an opt-in page for my free download," and the virtual assistant would have no idea what they were asking for, let alone how to do it!

Clients want to hire someone who understands: (1) what they are building in their business and (2) how they are doing it. Sounds so simple at face value, yet it is so very important.

The business model that we recommend and use with our online business clients is based on the product funnel model, as shown below. This relationship-based business model is an excellent way to build a sustainable and profitable online business.

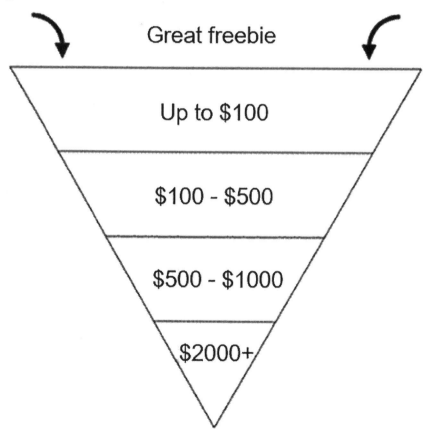

Figure 3.1 Product funnel model

Along with the business model you also need to know the **processes involved in implementing the client's various marketing and other business-building strategies.**

For example, one of the most common marketing strategies in the product funnel is to hold free training classes or webinars. If your client asked for support with this, would you know all the elements, steps and information required to setup, promote and execute a successful training?

There's more involved than you may think – here is a sample flowchart of just the first nine steps of the process:

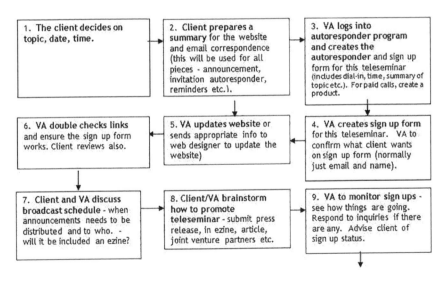

Figure 3.2 Sample flowchart

Your client is looking to you to take care of all the pieces, whether it's helping them set up a promotional webinar to creating a sales page for their new program. Even if you outsource the actual work (and I recommend that you do, but we'll talk more about that later), you need to understand and manage the complete process.

What is really required here is **training and experience**. The best (and probably the only) way to get a strong understanding of online-based business processes is through in-depth training and working with clients to apply them. We spend two full modules on business structures and process in our Certified OBM training (www.CertifiedOBM.com).

I was asked just the other day, "Tina, if I want to work as an OBM, should I first work as a virtual assistant?" And my answer was maybe.

If you are brand new to business and unsure about what you want to do, spending some time working as a virtual assistant is an excellent way to gain experience and learn the online industry. Learn about the process of launching a new product. Learn how to research and approach joint venture partners. Learn who to contact if your client wants to create a video promotion. Learn everything that you can! Working as a virtual assistant can give you a solid foundation to start working at the OBM level when you are ready.

If you are confident in your decision to start a business and your ability to work at the management level while learning the nuances of online business, then it may not be necessary to work as a VA at all. We have had many success people come from other careers, graduate from our Certified OBM training and go straight to working as an OBM for their clients.

Put simply, there are no rules. It's more about your goals and motivation. I know VAs who have reached the "bursting point" within a year and are more than ready to transition to an OBM role (should they wish to do so). For others it may take a few years before they feel they have the experience and confidence to take on this bigger role.

If you are new to this, go ahead and get started now in whatever capacity feels right for you. Be it starting out as a virtual assistant or diving straight into your training to become an Online Business Manager.

OBM as thought partner: Time to speak up!

We all know the value and importance of talking to others about business strategies and ideas. This is the reason people join mastermind groups, hire coaches and create business partnerships. Being a business owner can be a lonely job and I believe it is essential to have others with whom you can collaborate in order to create a successful and fulfilling business.

> **SIDENOTE**
>
> Having worked from home now since 1999, people often ask me "Aren't you lonely? I think I would get so lonely being at home by myself all day ..." The answer is no, not at all – for the simple fact that almost everything I do is in collaboration with someone else. Be it my team, my clients or my colleagues.
>
> My point here is this: I'm in touch with people pretty much every day, via email, phone or instant message. I'm never lonely. In fact, I have forged much stronger relationships online than I ever have working in the offline world. And these relationships are essential to my success – if I had to do it all on my own, it simply wouldn't happen.

Clients want someone to be a sounding board, to brainstorm with them, share ideas and consider options; someone who isn't afraid to speak up. When I talk to business owners, they describe this as their number one wish, "I would love to find someone who will brainstorm with me and help me figure things out." I call it a wish because most business owners have a really hard time finding someone who will do this with them and have had to "do without" – which means a HUGE opportunity for you!

What is required to be a thought partner? A couple of things; you need both **experience + confidence** to be able to effectively speak up with your clients.

Experience comes from having done 'it' before and knowing what's involved with a specific strategy or idea. You can share with your client, "I did X with another client and what happened was Y, so we may want to consider that here." or "I know X tried that once and it really worked, have you also considered doing Y?" The more specific experience we have, the more intelligently and effectively we can contribute to conversations with our clients.

More importantly, you need to **have confidence in yourself, your knowledge and your skill set.** "Getting lippy," with our clients, as I like to call it, does require a bit of sass on your part (heheh)! Some of us have to dig pretty deep to find this confidence; it's a very personal thing. The dictionary defines confidence as, "belief in oneself and one's powers or abilities."

As an OBM, that means that you believe in the value that you have to offer to your client's business. You aren't afraid to speak up and share your ideas, thoughts and experiences with your clients, or sometimes you ARE afraid but you do it anyways.

In my experience, confidence means that you are willing to contribute without letting the fear or worry of "am I offering value?" get in the way. Or put another way, you are willing to fall flat on your face, get up, shake it off and move on.

The thing is, that will rarely happen.

You see, clients are EAGER to hear from you. They want (and crave!) someone who is willing to engage, brainstorm and share ideas; someone who isn't afraid to challenge them at times, and even say "you are off your rocker here!"; someone who will speak up and tell them what they think (good, bad or otherwise). It is rare that I've heard of someone engaging with their clients at this level and getting put down for it. On the contrary, the clients are usually thrilled to have this kind of input as it is so rare for them to find it elsewhere.

This doesn't mean that you need to have all the answers (none of us do!). What it does mean is that you are willing to engage, with the intention that $1 + 1 = 3$, and that together with your client you can come up with so much more than either of you could ever do alone. **THAT is the heart of the OBM relationship.**

If the thought of speaking up makes you nervous, I invite you to explore that a bit further.

I find confidence is a cumulative thing, in both life and in business. We all start on the lesser side of confidence, and over time stretch ourselves in various ways that increase our confidence. And the more we stretch, the easier it is to continue to build confidence throughout our lives.

Confidence comes from doing what scares you. Go ahead and speak up, especially if the thought of doing so makes you cringe! A good exercise is to think of one of your clients and make a list of ideas that you have for growing their business. Then setup a time to talk with them about your ideas – just say "Sue, I was thinking about your business goals and wanted to share some ideas I had for accomplishing those goals." Most clients will be thrilled that you are thinking about their business growth and will gladly have a conversation with you.

Added value: Always looking for ways to market your client's business

Being that this is the marketing mindset, we naturally want to be looking for ways that we can help to build and grow (market!) our client's business.

The specific strategies will vary depending on the client's overall business plan and niche market. As an OBM you will want to be familiar with and/or practically experienced in all facets of Internet marketing including:

- Product planning and research
- Launch management
- Copywriting and content creation
- Advertising
- Website design and creation
- Search engine optimization
- Creation of graphics and user interface
- Shipping and fulfillment
- Traffic generation
- Conversion and
- The overall strategic marketing plan that creates a cohesive whole out of these elements

You may or may not be the one to do some of these marketing activities (depending on your background and strengths), however you DO need to understand Internet marketing and how all the pieces fit together.

As an OBM there are also some more subtle ways to look at marketing activities.

Whether it's for a specific product or promotion or just throughout the day, I like to ask myself, "What else can we do here?" There are quite often simple little things that can make a big difference in the long run, such as:

- Implementing an email signature that promotes your clients' free offers and/or products for sale (ensure everyone on the team is using the signatures)

- Creating an evergreen digital version of a live event or class to sell separately or as a package

- Creating a membership site to deliver classes, programs and products

- Adding an effective P.S. at the bottom of a sales page

- Making good use of the thank you page after purchase (prime real estate to get them to spend more)

- Making the Buy buttons on a sales page extra attractive and noticeable

- Creating an upsell on the order page for a product, for example, "Buy this book together with our workbook and save 15%"

- Putting a little extra "oomph" and adding keywords into the title of an article

- Introducing clients to each other so they can cross-promote

- Being on the lookout for new easy places to promote, advertise or find joint venture partners

- Adding more autoresponder messages that follow up with previous customers, so they are reminded to visit your client's offerings again

Calling the shots: Being a decision maker for the business

On a day-to-day basis there are many decisions to be made in any online based business: When do we want to send out this promotion? Who is going to fix the typo on our website? Where can we find someone to edit my book? How should I respond to this upset customer? What should our next new product offering be?

Without an OBM, most of these decisions fall squarely on the shoulders of business owners. As such, anytime there is a question, their team members will turn to them for the answer. Because most business owners are incredibly busy, this process results in delays and it can also feel like a hassle to have to deal with every little thing.

That's why our clients want someone who is willing and able to make decisions on their behalf, and not wait to run everything past them first. This doesn't mean that you will be making ALL decisions for your client, however you can certainly help with a lot of the tactical and operational decisions that come up on a day-to-day basis.

How do you know when to check with your client before making a decision?

Generally, any decisions about money or strategy should be run by your client. On the other hand, your client will probably be relieved once you take over some of the administrative, operational and customer service decisions. When you first start working with a new client, you will run a lot of things by them, as you get to know each other and build a level of trust that will give you more freedom in making decisions down the road.

You may also want to set some standards and procedures around this. For example, I once worked with a client whose policy was that her team could make a decision on refunds that would be less than $100, but anything over $100 had to be brought to her attention. A "Decision Making Standards" guide can be something that you create for your client and add to over time as reference for future decisions.

When you do need to approach your client for a decision, come to them with a proposed solution.

Let's say that you have an angry customer email that you aren't quite sure to handle. Instead of asking your client, "How do you want me to respond to this?" craft a potential response to the customer and send it to your client, asking, "I'm not quite sure how to respond to this. Will you check my proposed response below and let me know if this is OK or if you have changes?" Not only will your client love you for being proactive, you will also speed up the decision-making process as your client can review and respond much quicker than they can create their own response from scratch.

Be your client's personal first line of defense

Your job as the OBM is also to protect your client from certain decisions that your client should not be wasting his or her time on. This is especially important with operational and systems-based decisions.

Let's say your client wants to set up a new content marketing website. First, bring them a summary of options and ideas for them to consider and ask for their approval on the parameters of the project. While you are creating the website, do NOT go to them with every little question that you have ("Where do you want this link? Did you want me to add your picture here? Should I change this description to match your main website?").

Instead, go ahead and set up the new website based on your experience and then have your client look at a draft version and request any changes. Again, it is better to present them with a solution to review (a completed draft version) than to ask them what to do at every step along the way.

This is ESPECIALLY important for clients who enjoy systems and administrative tasks. If given the chance, these clients can very easily become involved in these things to the point of distraction. These clients may want to know more about the details than other clients would, but don't be afraid to lovingly "slap their wrist" if they try to become too involved. It is not the best use of their time to get too involved on the backend and you may need to remind them of that.

Becoming a part of the client's business

I have a coaching client who has been in business for over four years now and has several people on her team who have worked with her that entire time. We were talking recently about ways that she can get out of the day-to-day needs of her business, so she can focus more on growth activities. I asked about the current people on her team and whether any of them might be ready to take on a bigger role within her business. Her response:

"There is one girl I've worked with for years who does a great job, but she always refers to it as 'your business.' For example, she will say 'Here is an update for YOUR webpage' or 'What do YOU want to do here.' Never does she say OUR, US or WE when talking about the work we do together, even after all these years. I don't get the sense that she really cares about my business"

Can you see what my client is saying here? The words that her team member is using are drawing a line between her and the work she is doing for her client. She isn't really showing that she is engaged or invested in the work.

This is such an interesting distinction! On one hand I totally get why this is happening – after all, it isn't the team members business, so why should she act as though it is? This is how most contractors (and employees) act with our clients (and employers). We draw a line in the sand between the two of us, and I believe that's to keep ourselves safe from the impact our work has on our client's business.

We're not going to get deep into the psychology of why this happens, but I would really like to challenge this status quo way of working.

When a client hires us to work with them and contribute to their business is some way, it truly is a collaborative effort. Whether it's managing their schedule or helping them create a new product line, the end result is created together. While the client may own that result, energetically you are a part of it as well.

Look at the words you use when talking to or about your clients. Are you saying YOURS or OURS? YOU or WE? Pay attention to what you are saying or typing over the next few days and make note of it.

I challenge you to start using more inclusive language and pay attention to how that feels. Does it make you uncomfortable? If so, dig a little bit into that and see what's up. Perhaps you need to do a bit of personal work to feel comfortable with this level of engagement. It could be you feel you don't deserve it, or perhaps you truly don't have confidence in the work you do. Or maybe there is an issue with the client that you need to face. This can be a tough process indeed, but don't be afraid to shine that light on what is going on behind the scenes.

Being plugged in as a part of your client's business is essential to working in an OBM capacity. If you can't do that then this may not be the best role for you.

CHAPTER 4

WHAT SETS YOU APART– A COACHING APPROACH

It's not always about what you do, but how you do it.

There is a subtle skill in working as an OBM that will really help you connect and grow with your clients, what we call the Coaching Approach. Not only was Andrea Lee my partner in launching the Certified OBM Training back in 2009, she is also one of the finest coaches that I know, and I was thrilled when she agreed to write this chapter! So allow me to pass the mic to Andrea here for a short while.

When Tina asked me to contribute this chapter to her book, I had to smile to myself a little. Little did she know how much of what I'd write would be a direct result of my experience of what she brings to the world: stellar, steadfast and superhuman-seeming business management of the online endeavours we've collaborated on for well over a decade now. It's little wonder that our initial working relationship has become a once-in-a-lifetime friendship and lifelong collaboration of projects and ideas.

There is a simple example that will begin to show you why this chapter is an important part of this book, and it has to do with things going wrong. Although the rest of this book will, I believe, become a textbook for the ages to guide you through the territory of online business management, there are still, to be blunt, a lot of potential pitfalls you will want to be on the alert for.

Which is where a so-called "coaching approach" comes in, and it will be especially useful to you for the very reason that there are so many unknowns on planet OBM.

So just what is this thing we're calling a coaching approach? Consider this:

You are an Online Business Manager for an industry leader who's got some very big business growth in the works. One of their key projects has you in charge of a team of two virtual assistants. One of them, let's call her Randy, had a deadline last week that she hasn't met. She's been saying she's on top of it but you're getting a wonky feeling about it – it doesn't smell right to you.

Turns out, you're right. You use your project management, operations management and people management skills (that you will be learning about in the next chapters) and sort out that basically, Randy has dropped the ball big time. The work isn't done.

But even worse than that, she's led you to believe it's been fine the whole time when the fact of the matter is, she was stuck, didn't ask for help, and let things get completely out of hand before "'fessing up" when you confronted her. She probably didn't even understand what was required of her in the first place. Not a pretty sight, and in some ways, something that can only happen this drastically because of the online nature of the team. In other words, the kind of mess an OBM can either sink or swim in.

You know the kind of the cleanup they have to do at the fish market after a busy morning? Yep. Bad.

So as the Online Business Manager in this scenario, what do you do? You have any number of choices available – what does your instinct tell you? Take a moment to listen in to your rational mind telling you, "I'd do step one, two and then three," while your emotions are saying "Oh, crap."

The coaching approach aside for the moment, clearly you will have some concrete, nuts and bolts things to do, just as any manager would – whether they are in HR for a law firm or the head server at a pub. What's the extent of the damage? Does the person need to be taken off the project, rapido, or will you have them clean it up? How is your client impacted and can they immediately be cared for and retained? Who on the team could step up into the situation and pinch hit?

You need to go beyond the practical

The heart of a coaching approach goes beyond all these reasonable and practical management skills. It goes to the idea that wherever something great is being achieved, a coaching approach is in there somewhere. And that wherever a coaching approach is used, a greater degree of success will follow.

Coaching is ...

A questioning approach towards thinking, living and communicating that improves everything.

Applying the coaching approach to our fish market scenario, after the dust has settled it might look like this:

COACHING APPROACH TACTIC #1: Assume everyone is doing their very best, especially when they don't seem like it.

This means that even though the Virtual Assistant crashed and burned, there is a story behind it. Not even just that their dog is ill, or they're overworked, either. Very often it can mean that (1) expectations of the project weren't clear in the beginning (2) they did not realize they were welcome to ask "stupid" questions (3) prior experience on projects for this business had deadlines that were flexible or even (4) their self-esteem is low for unrelated reasons and they aren't good at setting personal boundaries or saying no.

COACHING APPROACH TACTIC #2: Set up a business culture that requires over-communication, always. And that the only real mistake that can occur is the failure to communicate early.

In an online business situation, the majority of unknown "gotcha's" will be prevented with the application of this one coaching approach tactic. I've been known to get very adamant when emphasizing this one, along the lines of:

"You can't get it wrong UNLESS you don't tell me you're getting it wrong." Translation? **The only real mistake is a failure to communicate.** You can call me up in the middle of the night and tell me things are doing horribly, and really, I will be much more okay with it than not knowing until it's too late.

COACHING APPROACH TACTIC #3: Be serenely confident in the fact that until you successfully go through a conflict or sensitive negotiation with someone, you don't know the true nature of the relationship.

I am of the conviction that until you go through a tough or even just touchy something with someone, you aren't really friends. Perhaps because Tina and I only ever work with clients we respect as much as our friends, we apply this to our business relationships too.

As an OBM who's in it for the long haul and wants to really reach the pinnacle of success available, be open and willing to embrace conflict. Take feedback as a vitamin and strengthen your internal self each time. Use the other coaching approach tactics here to anchor your conflict in productive conversation. Remember that to the degree you can be serene through a conflict, the more you are learning and the less likely you'll have to go through this same conflict again, in another form.

How does this apply in our scenario? In mentoring OBMs over the years, we've come to recognize that managing conflict is one of the most difficult things an OBM does. Your goal is to be able to transcend the fear of initiating, quickly, the conversations that need to happen with the errant VA and also of presenting the ugly problem to your client.

COACHING APPROACH TACTIC #4: Come to understand that the business can only grow to the extent, and at the rate that, the business owner grows as a person.

I call this the "Paul Principle," in sharp contrast to the "Peter Principle" which says that in corporations, people will rise to the level of their incompetency and then stay there. Likewise, in any given business, the growth of the business will rise or fall to the level of the business owner's personal development. If a business owner isn't willing to look themselves in the mirror and acknowledge their whole selves, experience says the business won't be able to make big shifts either.

Applying this once again to our scenario, let's use our imaginations to illustrate this tactic.

Is it possible that the business owner has made a habit of requesting to start lots of new projects at the last minute, within short timeframes, only to abandon them later, making deadlines moot (and downright annoying)?

Is it possible the business owner "owed" something to the virtual assistant and didn't follow through, preventing the VA from being able to proceed and leaving the VA feeling unable to speak "truth to power" out of fear?

Could we consider the fact that the business owner is someone of such high profile that the VA has put herself in a state of ultra-sensitivity, worrying about her performance and in awe about her association with this person, resulting in her being paralyzed and stuck?

Especially when it comes to the online world, these are the subtexts that can often emerge ONLY when a coaching-approach is taken. Based on the scenario and tactics above,

I hope you're beginning to grasp what it means to take a coaching approach as an Online Business Manager. It can be boiled down to something very simple:

It's not only what you do but HOW you do it that will set you apart.

So how do you translate this into the way of being that is the heart of what an Online Business Manager is?

There's no requirement that you become a coach or take coach training, however if you do it will without question better equip you for your OBM career as well as transform your life. Start with the basic tenet that underlines everything coaching:

Questions.

Lead with questions.

In case of emergency, ask the very best questions you have.

Ask what questions you're not asking and what those will reveal.

Which brings us to...

COACHING APPROACH TACTIC #5: Recognize that a business is one of the world's most effective vehicles for personal transformation there is.

As an Online Business Manager, the trials and tribulations you go through as you invest in the vision of your clients will coach you, if you let them.

One of your clients is taking a sabbatical for three months and you will earn considerably less. Have you become a little complacent about your work as an OBM and what will this 3-month window allow you to do, or become, as a person and a professional?

The business is taking a new turn and you don't have the specialized expertise required. Is this an opportunity for you to release your preference to be the one who knows everything? Can your identity as a success survive the fact that you won't be the smart one in this scenario?

You're in a low energy mood for a while and you realize it's because you're tired of using a coaching approach with your client! Instead, you turn it on yourself and ask yourself where are you not stretching?

The ways in which a coaching approach can be applied to your path as an OBM are limitless. In fact, I would encourage you not to think of a coaching approach as something you turn on and off, or as a blanket you put on top of something. It's the inner fuel that drives the work, not decoration.

As you read on in the chapters that follow, I know you'll benefit beyond measure from what is provided as concrete direction for how to play a bigger role with your clients and yourself. Read and listen closely and you'll see a coaching approach between the lines, and that this theme runs as a thread throughout the OBM conversation. In fact, I'll go so far as to say that quite possibly, without a coaching approach to business, the OBM role would not have emerged quite this way!

The very best OBMs are an embodiment of the coaching approach and speaking as a business owner, I'm incredibly grateful for this.

I hope you don't mind if I say on behalf of the business owners whose lives and business you will touch, thank you, for your willingness to wade into these uncharted waters.

You're about to enter into the guts of the "doing" part of the book, where the "what you do" steps are revealed. As you soak in the wisdom there, read with a coaching approach in mind. And when you're ready to apply a coaching approach in real-life, here are some sample questions you can refer back to:

- As we talk about X (where X is a new project, idea, problem that needs solving), what happens in your physical body?

- Why do you think X is happening? (Where X is a recurring problem, results that aren't as stellar as hoped, an emotional reaction on the part of the client)

- Would you prefer to earn more money and work a little more, or earn about the same amount of money and work a lot less?

- What is the end goal of your business – is it to work it until you retire at a certain time? Sell it to someone for a lump sum? Have it be run by a team while you pursue other interests?

- What other area of your life have you experienced success in? What can you transfer from that success and apply to your business? (A person trained in martial arts might recognize they aren't being as strict or disciplined with themselves in their business as they can be and can enjoy being.)

CHAPTER 5

DRIVING THE BUS - PROJECT MANAGEMENT

Clients want someone to help ensure that things get done

As a business grows, it becomes more and more important to have someone who is staying on top of everything to make sure it gets done (this person is traditionally called a project or general manager in a corporate business setting).

According to Wikipedia, *project management* is the **discipline** of **planning, organizing, and managing** resources to bring about the successful completion of specific project goals and objectives.

Many business owners are horrible project and team managers (or they really don't enjoy it). They started their business because they wanted to offer their expertise to the world, not so they could run a business. They are either tolerating a role that they really don't like doing or they are having a hard time getting things done at all. They want and need someone to come in and take control of the various projects and elements of their business, to ensure that things run smoothly and get done in a timely matter.

I like to call this **driving the bus**. It is our clients who determine where the bus needs to go (the result you are working towards), but it is up to the OBM to make sure that we get there.

With this role you are taking a heavy load off the client's shoulders. They no longer need to be the one to constantly manage all the people and tasks involved in completing projects. Instead, **they can focus their time and energy on growing the business and serving clients.**

Your responsibility here is simple – get stuff done! I can't tell you how many times I've spoken to business owners who have loads of projects in various stages of completion that are just sitting there and rotting away, for the simple fact that they are either too busy or too distracted to see things through to the end. It's literally like a goldmine hiding just a foot under the ground, ready for someone to discover it and bring its wealth to the world.

That's why a good OBM truly is "worth their weight in gold" to the client.

> **SIDENOTE**
>
> I purposely take a simplified view of project management. An in-depth overview of project management would go into much more than I cover here – milestones, Gantt charts and such. While necessary in the huge projects that large corporations tackle, most OBMs are working on projects that are smaller and simpler in scope.
>
> To me the heart of project management is "getting stuff done in the simplest way possible." Sometimes the more complex philosophies, steps and tools can get in the way of that and create a new pile of work themselves. There is certainly nothing wrong with using project management methodologies and tools, just be sure that they are helping projects move forward and not causing confusion or delay for you, the client or the team.

Are project managers born or created?

Ahhh, the age-old question of nature or nurture. I'm certainly not claiming to have an answer, just a perspective. From what I've seen, some people are great at project management; usually those who are naturally organized, able to 'see all the pieces' and have a track record of moving things along to completion. Other people may fall flat. They may be good at getting their own stuff done, but not good at pulling together all the people and pieces required to get a bigger project done.

How do you know if you're a good project manager? Take on a project and see if it gets done. The proof is in the pudding, as they say.

In some cases, you may need more experience to hone your project management skills and with a few projects under your belt you could become an excellent project manager. It's like you have a dormant gene that – once activated – kicks into high gear and away you go.

The key quality of a good project manager is that they don't shy away from the responsibility. They are willing to take on a project and know that they are accountable for whether or not it gets done. They need to be energized by this responsibility, not paralyzed by it (though a bit of fear is OK, so long as it motivates you in a positive way).

Let's take a closer look at what exactly project management is:

Discipline

Discipline – how I love that word. At face value it sounds almost harsh and punitive, but discipline means honouring a commitment. If you say you are going to do something, then you do it. You own the responsibility of getting something done. It's up to you.

This is where most projects fall apart. After all, it can be easy to plan something, organize and even get started. However, without discipline it can be just as easy to let things slide and never reach completion.

In best practices you really do need to **have one person be the project manager** – not having a designated "owner" for a project generally means that it won't get done. I've seen it time and time again. There may be plenty of people on the bus, but no one is driving it.

This happens a lot in small business teams, for the simple fact that so many of us are used to working alone and doing everything ourselves.

Planning

Before starting any project, you want to make sure you plan to prevent frustration and wasted time and resources along the way.

Let's look at an example. Your client has just written a book and needs to get a sales page "live" so he can start selling the book.

The first step is to plan the sales page, which means getting really clear on what exactly your client wants.

- Is there an example of a sales page that he really likes? Which elements does he like or not like? I always like to work from an example, especially if your client is new to sales pages or really wants to try something different.

- Does he want a short/sweet style sales page or a longer/harder sell page?
- What domain name does he want for the sales page?
- Will you need to hire a copywriter to write the page?
- Will there be any video on the page?
- Do you need a 3D graphic of the book to put on the page?
- What look (colours, graphics, layout) does he want for the page?
- Does he have testimonials ready or do you need to collect some?
- What price will the book sell for? Is it an e-book or print book?
- Are there any bonuses to go along with the purchase?
- Is there going to be a special launch price/offer?
- Does your client want an upsell as part of the buying process (e.g., Buy the book and workbook for a discounted price)?
- Does he want to promote the book through JV Partners and Affiliates?

As you can see, to effectively plan this project, you need to have a strong understanding of all the elements of setting up a sales page. If you don't have experience in this yet, you will need to do some research or invest in some training to get you up to speed.

You will also want to consider the cost of each piece of the project so that you can a) have a good idea of what the overall cost will be, b) prevent last minute surprises and c) have a guideline for keeping costs in check.

Organizing

You've planned out the project and all the requirements, now it's time to start organizing all the pieces. In the online business world this generally means that you will be hiring contractors to complete various parts of the project. In our sales page example, you may need:

- A copywriter to create the words
- A graphic designer to create a header and/or 3D graphic of the book
- A web designer or techie VA to create the page
- A VA to set up the Buy button and link it to the shopping cart
- A VA to coordinate collection of testimonials and bonus items.

There may be certain elements that you are going to do yourself, as well.

You will also want to have a timeline for when you need each element completed, so you can coordinate with vendors on when you need their piece completed. For example, you will need the copywriter and designer to be finished before the web designer can create the page.

Managing

You've laid the foundation (planning) and organized all your resources (people); now it's time to get to work. This is where the management piece comes in, which is perhaps the most important part of the process.

When I was still working as an OBM I would joke and say," I'm a professional nag," but in some ways I wasn't really joking. This is where an OBM spends a lot of energy day-to-day – checking in with people to ensure that their part of the project is moving along and will be completed on time (or not, in which case adjustments need to be made).

I've found that most people need a bit of a "loving nag" from time to time to get stuff done. It's just human nature; if we don't have someone stressing the importance of getting X done (nagging us), then it can be very easy for us to let X slide a bit and not complete it. This is especially important when working with contractors who have a bunch of different clients and projects on the go. Think about it – if you have four design projects on your plate and you KNOW that I'm going to be asking you for mine (versus another client who may not nag quite so much), whose project are you going to work on first? Probably mine, so you can get me out of your hair.

We assume that people will get stuff done when they say they will, but this isn't always true. It's not that people are bad or lazy. In fact, it's usually quite the opposite with most contractors that I've had the pleasure to work with. They are SO busy that they have a tough time getting everything done in the time that they promised. They don't mean to be late with a project; they are just struggling to complete something for you and 10 other people at the same time. Well, as the saying goes – the squeaky wheel gets the grease – so don't be shy when it comes to checking in with them and "nagging" a bit as needed.

How do you nag? It's simple, really. If I want to check-in with a contractor on the status of a project, I will send an email or an instant message that says something like:

Hi Ben,

Just checking on the status of the social media graphics you are working on for us. Do you have a draft ready for our review?

Thanks!

Or if it was due yesterday and I haven't received it yet, I might say:

Hi Ben,

Just checking on the status of the social media graphics you are working on for us. You were going to have them ready for us yesterday. If you already sent them over I may have missed that email, do you mind resending?

If they aren't not ready yet, can you give me an ETA on completion? As you know, we have promotions starting in a couple of days and we need to have the graphics asap.

Thanks!

It is especially important to not let emotions come into play here, even when you are feeling frustrated because someone is late with something or if you've emailed them five times and aren't getting an answer. People will usually respond in kind, so if you get nasty with them chances are they will get nasty with you. And when that happens, I can almost guarantee that your projects will fall to the bottom of their list.

Remember, being late usually isn't anything personal; it's just a result of the contractor being overwhelmed with work themselves. A little compassion can go a long way. If I know that a contractor is really struggling with everything on their plate and I have some "wiggle room" on my end, I like to be able to take a bit of pressure off for them.

Suzy, I know you are swamped right now. We are OK to wait until Friday for the new banner if that helps. Let me know, thanks!

It's this kind of consideration that will pay dividends in the long run, as you build strong relationships with your contractors and stay at the top of their list for future projects.

The key to nagging is to do it! Check in with people on a regular basis (daily is good, hourly is too much). If it's super important I may even reach out again later in the day if they haven't responded to an earlier message that I sent. And if I'm desperate I'll pick up the phone and call (which I rarely have to do).

SIDENOTE

Andrea has an excellent strategy that she uses when she is waiting get a response from someone, what I like to call her "bait and catch" strategy. She will send someone a message, something like "Which of these graphics do you prefer?" When she gets a response to that it's a signal that the person is online now, so she quickly sends another message about a matter she's been waiting for an answer about.

She has "caught" the person online, the virtual equivalent of catching someone in their office. The person can't simply brush her off and pretend that they aren't online. Quite often she will finally get a response to the other matter she has been waiting on, for the simple fact that they can't hide from her at that moment.

Or, better yet (sneaky her), sometimes she even puts two items into one message. One item is something she knows the person will reply to, something juicy like a win or celebration, and the other item is the request. Hey, whatever works that's civilized and respectful is okay in my books.

The key here is that your "bait" message is very simple, something they can read and respond to right away. If you send a bait message that is more than a quick read, then chances are they will just let it sit in their Inbox along with your other requests. In fact, you'll learn very quickly that short messages are the way to go overall.

Three strikes and you're out!

If you don't get a response after three tries within three days, then I would look for someone else to complete that task for you. It's one thing for someone to be running late and let you know about it, it's a whole other thing to be ignored. I won't tolerate that and will quickly cut those contractors loose.

Clients need nagging too

Don't be afraid to nag your clients too! Most clients really want someone to nag them to get things done, and in fact OBMs have been hired for just this reason. As one client so delicately put it, "Tina, I know that you are like a bulldog with a bone – you just don't let go. And I need someone like that to keep me on task." Strange as it may seem, this was quite a compliment in my books.

Sometimes our client can be the biggest barrier to getting a project complete, except now we can't use the three strikes rule (LOL). You can nag your clients, of course, but here are three other things you can do to make projects easier for them to complete.

1. Start it for them

Get something started for your client – write a promotional email for example - and then they'll take it from there and tweak or edit as they see fit. It is scientifically proven that starting something is what requires the most energy, but that once you get going it doesn't take near as much energy to keep going. Your clients are busy enough; get their project started and it will take a lot less of their time and energy to take it through to completion.

> **SIDENOTE**
>
> Don't get offended if your client takes a writing project that you start and totally changes it. This generally isn't a reflection of the quality of your work, it is more to do with the client wanting to write "in their own voice," or that they have simply decided to talk about something else. It's never personal, so

don't take it to heart. And just the same way that a married couple starts to finish each other's sentences over time, you will soon be able to write in your client's voice without even thinking about it.

2. Ping-pong it

If your client has started something and is stuck with it, ask them if you can take a stab at it for them. Sometimes a fresh eye and new perspective is all that is needed to get something done. You can look at what they've done so far, add your bit to it and send it back to them to jump into again. This may go back and forth a few times, which is why we call it the ping-pong strategy. This is a HIGHLY effective way to get the momentum going on something that is just sitting there stuck for whatever reason.

3. Ask them what they need

I've found that sometimes a task may not be complete for the simple fact that the client needs something to finish it, and they are either too busy or distracted to remember that they can ask for your help.

For example, your client may be working on copy for a sales page, and they want to quote something from a book they read recently but can't find the book on their shelf. You could easily do a bit of research and find the quote for them, so they can get it done. When you do a little bit of digging you may find that your client is stuck by something that could be easily handled on your end, and you are able to quickly fix it so they can keep on moving.

Helping them to let go

> *"People do what they do because they have*
> *nothing more compelling to do."*
>
> - Thomas Leonard

Most business owners are used to doing everything themselves, and there are some that may have a tough time letting go of making sure that things get done. They may be constantly looking over your shoulder, asking for updates on every little piece, wanting to approve each step and essentially driving you nuts!

When you are new to working with a client or to doing a particular project for them then it is certainly natural for them to be more closely involved as part of the training process. But there comes a time when the client needs to step back and let you do what they've hired you to do. Otherwise the work will be highly frustrating for you, and it can be tough for you to get any work done.

When you first start working with a client they may have **Lone Ranger Syndrome.**

Even though they very clearly want and need help in the management and completion of projects, they are used to being intimately involved and may find it tough to not be plugged into the process. They are used to being a Lone Ranger in their business and knowing everything that is going on, and they are finding it a hard habit to break.

Lone Rangers generally just need some time to build trust in you – they need to see that you can create results so that they can let go of the need to "know it all." If you simply do your job and understand your client's need to check in on your results, then over time they will get less and less involved as they trust that you will handle things. Some clients may end up with a bunch of free time that they don't know what to do with, and it's your job to gently remind them to work on business-building activities, the things that they wished they had time to do before you came along; anything that only THEY can do.

If your client gets really stuck here, you may want to suggest that they hire a business coach to help them decide where to best focus their time and energy in this stage of business growth.

If you have worked together for a while and your client is still not letting go then you may have a **Control Freak** on your hands.

At first you may not be able to tell that a client is a Control Freak, but it will become clear after you've proven yourself several times to be competent, yet they still want to be involved in every little thing. I would suggest that you first have a conversation with your client, and simply point out that they've hired you to do this job for them and it is not the best use of their time to still be so involved. Ask them what they need to let go and trust that you will be able to take care of things for them.

If things don't change after having this conversation, then this could be a VERY tough situation to work with as an OBM, as you will essentially be doing double-duty of managing all of the pieces and keeping your client updated on all the pieces as well.

In our experience there isn't much you can do to change this in your client, as it is usually something quite deeply ingrained and beyond the scope of an OBM to handle or fix. You may very well have to cut them loose at some point; it is near impossible to truly help someone take their business to the next level when they aren't willing to let go. Save your gifts for those who will use them.

CHAPTER 6

STREAMLINE AND AUTOMATE - OPERATIONS MANAGEMENT

Clients want someone to setup systems that ensure
their business runs smoothly

One of the keys to growth is to set up a solid foundation of business systems and standards. Without it a business can only grow so far and may in fact fall apart like a deck of cards.

I'm reminded of a fulfillment house that we used to use for our book shipments. When we first started using them they were a smaller company, the type where you could email them and it would be the owner who replied. As time went on we could see that they were becoming busier and growing by leaps and bounds. Then, suddenly one day they shut down – no warning, just an email that stated they were no longer in business.

What happened? From what we could tell they had simply grown too fast, and their infrastructure couldn't handle it. Such a shame really, when the dream of any business owner is to keep on growing. But without a solid foundation, that growth may turn into a nightmare.

This is where the OBM comes in, ensuring that all business systems, procedures and tools are in place and functioning smoothly to the benefit of the business.

Standard operating procedures

A great starting point is to help your clients put together a Standard Operating Procedures guide (what we like to call a SOP). As a business grows, it is essential to have a central how-to guide for handling everything that needs to be done. How are orders processed? What are the proper responses to various customer service enquiries? Where are the websites hosted and how do you update the sites?

We highly recommend using an online tool such as Teamwork Projects to create an SOP. This will give everyone a central, online location for accessing the guide when needed (versus having a Word document that lives on someone's computer). Plus, this system acts as a project management tool where you will create projects, set milestones, and create tasks, and it is very easy to update and will track when changes are made and by whom. Teamwork.com has a great notification system and will send everyone an email update when something is new or changed (so you don't have to send updates manually).

Here is a screenshot of the SOP Guide Template that we give to all of our Certified OBMs.

Figure 6.1 Screenshot of SOP

Creating an SOP is a great first OBM project with your clients. Most small business owners don't have an SOP in place. They understand the importance of having such a guide, especially as they grow and continue to bring more people onto their team. However, they haven't had the time or inclination to put one together themselves (for most business owners this would be a daunting task, nor is it the best use of their time). Having someone take on the task of creating an SOP is a huge relief to them.

Really, a business is not grown up until they have an SOP in place – it is that important to a growing business and thus a worthy project for any OBM to tackle. The SOP becomes your touchstone for success in managing operations. As the business grows you always want to ensure that you have the latest systems in place AND that they are being tracked and managed via the SOP.

Automate, automate, automate

When a business owner wants to expand his or her business the first thing they usually think of is growing their team. This is certainly part of growth and we will discuss expanding the team in our next chapter.

But before doing any hiring you need to first look at the client's business systems and processes. Chances are that there are some things that you would hire for that could be automated instead.

I recommend automating over hiring any day for a few reasons:

- Automating a process means less room for errors and delays.
- You will generally pay less for an automated system than you will for a person to do the same task.
- Automating certain tasks (especially tedious tasks) frees up the team to focus on other business

building tasks – a benefit to both the client and the team members (who may be getting bored with these types of tasks).

For example, Andrea and I once made a change to how we process orders for our print book *Money, Meaning and Beyond*.

Our old system required that we purchase a bunch of books up front and ship them to our fulfillment warehouse for storage. Then, as orders were processed in our shopping cart system our VA would export those orders and then manually upload them to the fulfillment house once a week for shipping.

Then we switched to using a "print on demand" supplier for our book, which has made this entire process much easier. Thanks to the wonderful folks at Vervante.com, we now have an automated system that connects directly to our shopping cart. Now, when a book order comes into our cart it is set to notify Vervante to produce a book and ship it out. There is no need for our VA to do anything at all anymore, nor any delays on shipping or missed orders as everything happens automatically with each order. So nice!

The three key benefits of this change have been:

- We save the upfront cost of maintaining a stock of print books.

- We save the cost to store those books at a fulfillment warehouse.

- We no longer have to rely on a VA to manually process the orders for shipping; everything happens automatically between our shopping cart and Vervante, even if the VA is sick or on holidays.

See how a simple, automated system can make a notable difference? This simple change required less of the VA's time, resulting in lower costs for manual tasks and an overall higher profit margin. Now that's the power of automation at work.

Check The OBM Toolbox at the back of this book for a list of recommended tools and systems.

How do you decide what to automate in your client's business? Here are some questions that will help:

What 'tedious' tasks are your clients and/or their team spending a lot of time on?

I find that the tedious tasks are usually the ones that are easiest to automate. Posting consistently to social media is a good example. Most clients want to do some form of social media marketing and will quite often delegate this task to a VA on their team. Depending on how many social media platforms they are using, scheduling a single post can take a VA up to an hour or more! Plus, most VAs really don't enjoy this task, and it may fall to the bottom of their list and in some cases not get done at all.

There are some great social media scheduling systems available now that will automate this process for you, like Meet Edgar or Hootsuite. You just enter your article once and these systems blast out the post to a bunch of social media platforms. Some of these platforms allow you to set up queues or libraries of posts that can be recycled according to a schedule. This frees your VA to focus on other business-building activities for you.

It is especially important to see what kinds of tedious tasks your client is doing themselves. Again, we want to always be trying to take things off our clients' plates, so they can focus on the more important business-building activities that only THEY can do.

I once worked with a client who was manually entering names into her database every time she attended a networking event and came back with a bunch of business cards. Eek! First of all, she shouldn't be the one entering those names into the database as it wasn't a good use of her time. And more importantly, how could this be automated? We created a system to scan the business cards instead so that they would be automatically loaded up to the database. What used to take an hour (or more!) now took only minutes to complete.

Are there ongoing errors or delays occurring anywhere in your business?

One of my clients ran a 6-month coaching program and asked each member of the program to read and agree to a set of standards to complete their registration. She would send a PDF form for her coaching clients to print, read, sign and fax back. Then, a VA would gather the faxes, enter the client contact information into a spreadsheet and send the client a Welcome package. This was a lot of work for the VA to coordinate and created a gap between when a person would send in their fax and when they would receive their Welcome packet (sometimes a day or so, depending on how busy the VA was).

To simplify the process, we set up an online agreement form. Now, when someone registers for the program they are taken to a webpage with an online agreement form that they can immediately read and "sign" (by submitting their name). Once they submit their name, they gain immediate access to the program. What was a 7-step and labour-intensive process that took days, is now a simple, three-step process that takes minutes and is easier for everyone involved.

Put yourself in your customer's shoes and ask: is there anything in your buying process that could be simpler, quicker or more pleasant?

As we got a glimpse of in the last example, automated systems can also make it much easier for customers to engage with your client, which is VERY important for the success of their business. You want to make it very easy for customers to buy, and automated systems will make the buying process smooth and enjoyable for all concerned.

I'm sure you have come across a situation like this – you are on a website and like what they have to offer. You go to click the Buy button and on the next page you're directed to print out an order form and fax it in, or to call in your order.

Now I don't know about you, but they have just lost my sale (unless I REALLY want what they have to offer). I don't want to spend the time to print out a form, fill it in by hand, fax it in and wait to get a response or confirmation of my order. Nor do I want to pick up the phone and wait for service or delay my order because I'm surfing in the off hours (as I often do). I'm ready to make my purchase now and would willingly submit my credit card number to do it. I want to order and pay and get immediate confirmation of my order. And in the case of downloadable products, I want instant access.

The more steps you ask a potential client to take to purchase, the less likely they will be to complete the sale. Look to automate and simplify the buying process as much as possible. An online shopping cart system is a definite must if you are selling online.

In a nutshell the name of the game is simple:

Is there a better way to do this?

This isn't just a one-time thing; it is something that you will always be doing as an OBM. In fact, you may want to commit to reviewing your entire Standard Operating Procedures guide at least once a year – we call this a Better Way Audit. There are always new online systems and tools that may make it possible to automate something you're doing manually. Ask yourself (as well as your "front line" team members), "Is there a better way to do this?"

SIDENOTE

There are two types of online tools out there: those built for corporations and those built for small business. In my experience the main difference is the cost – something created for big corporate business will always cost a lot more than something built for individuals or small business, even if they do the exact same thing! A good example is a Customer Relationship Management (CRM) system. Salesforce.com is a popular system that can cost hundreds of dollars per month. By comparison, Pipedrive is a simplified CRM system (perfect for the less complex needs of online business owners) and its price starts at $12.50 per month. Most corporate tools have features that the small business owner doesn't need and therefore shouldn't have to pay for.

> I remember when one of our favorite online calendars went "big business." We had been spending $97 per year for a small business subscription, but when they decided to change their target market to bigger companies that need online scheduling capabilities, they started charging $99 per month! It was the same system, just a different target market that would pay more. Needless to say, we decided to find another tool that was more in line with our needs and budget. The moral of this story is that if you find an online tool that looks great but costs a lot, keep digging because chances are there is a less expensive option that can do the same thing.

It is also important to plan for continued business growth and to act as though your client is a big company (even if they aren't yet).

If you look for systems that have varying packages and options that can grow with the business, this can save you the stress of having to switch systems down the road. As an example, to help one of my clients look more professional, we signed her up for a toll-free phone number. The toll-free service provider offers lots of bells and whistles – including sending an audio file of any calls received. We started using simplest options;

Becoming an Online Business Manager

however everything was ready to go for when my client needs to add additional extensions or to forward calls to a team member.

Automating is one of my favorite things about working online. Anything that will take a task off my plate is ideal in my mind.

96

CHAPTER 7

BUILDING THE TEAM - PEOPLE MANAGEMENT

Clients want someone to help build and manage their virtual team

---

In the virtual world, most clients rely on a team of contractors to support their business, and may only start hiring employees once they are in the 7-figure range. Even though hiring is a fact of life when it comes to owning a business, I have yet to meet a small business owner who enjoys the process of finding, hiring and managing their team. Many business owners have gone through the process of finding and hiring (usually a VA or a web designer) and in many cases have struggled to make it work. They know they need a team to help in various areas, but they do not enjoy the process of hiring and delegating. This is a huge area of need for most business owners, and the role of the OBM is highly important here.

Keeping it lean

As discussed in the last chapter, I'm a huge fan of automating before you hire. As such, I tend towards hiring a smaller, leaner team for my clients. The core team of key people will generally consist of the business owner (your client), the OBM (you) and one or more VAs. Depending on the business there may also be a delivery team, such as a group of associate coaches who help the client run their programs.

Outside of this key team there will be a number of contractors that you will call on from time to time for various projects. This may include copywriters, web designers, graphic designers, SEO professionals, internet marketing strategists, content managers, higher level technical support and more. Part of the beauty of working online is that there are so many wonderful contractors out there who can step in on an "as needed" basis. Gone are the days when anyone has to do it all. Now a business owner can have a core team, and then turn to specialists in these various areas when the business requires it.

"The more complex anything is, the more chances there are for something small to make it go off course"
- Andrea J. Lee

In my experience, if there are too many people on the core team it can make for a very confusing and overly busy environment. Like having too many cooks in the kitchen, when there are too many people on the core team they can end up stepping all over each other and nothing gets done. Plus, the more people there are on the core team, the more diluted the responsibility becomes. An ideal team has only a few people at the core who are responsible for getting stuff done and for managing the other contractors who are doing the work.

Let's use the example of a weekly core team meeting, which we highly recommend. I'm not a fan of meetings for the sake of meetings but a weekly touch-base meeting for the core team is essential. Even though we rely on various online tools for most of our day-to-day communication, nothing can take the place of a live conversation to keep the big picture alive.

As a three-way call between you (the OBM), your client (the business owner) and a VA, this meeting can be a quick and efficient way to get updates on projects, go over details of what's coming up, etc. But as you bring other people into the meeting, it starts to muddy the waters. For example, not everyone needs to know the specific tasks that the web designer is working on – it will confuse people and bring them into conversations that they have no role in. It's far better to meet weekly with the core team, who can then turn around and update peripheral team members.

As the OBM you want to work with your client to help define, source, hire, train and manage team members.

1. Defining

Defining the team is looking at the business needs and identifying what kind of help is needed. This is where your expertise will come in, as you need to know enough about the process of doing business online to know what kind of help you need to hire. It is VERY important to know exactly what you are hiring someone to do, to prevent confusion down the road on both sides.

For example, say you want to create a video for your client to put up on their homepage. Does the person you're hiring need to do everything from A-Z (identify the content, create the content, produce the video, edit it and coordinate with your web developer to put it on the homepage)? Or will your client record the video with their webcam and you just need someone to add an intro and convert it into a format that you can put online? There's a significant difference between those two jobs.

Once you are clear on the needs of the business you can look at putting together job descriptions for people you need to hire. Don't be intimidated by the terminology – in the online world it doesn't need to be a standard corporate 5-page job description - you just need to outline the skills, responsibilities and availability that you are looking for.

It is also a good idea to define how much you are willing to pay as contractor rates can vary greatly depending on skillset and level of experience.

2. Sourcing

Once you've defined the needs, it is the responsibility of the OBM to look for people to fill those roles. We are asked all the time how business owners can find people to join their team. We always recommend that you look first to your own network – start with who you know. If you need someone to create a video for you, simply send a note to your network asking if anyone knows a good vide producer. 90% of the time someone will have a recommendation of someone they have used themselves or heard good things about. Likewise, they may also be able to warn you against using certain people and save you some potential headache.

Over time, as an OBM you will develop your own core team of contractors who you've used for projects in the past. I had my own rolodex of specialists in various areas who I could call on to use with any of my OBM clients – I knew them, trusted their work and because we had an established relationship they were quite responsive to my needs and would often "bump me up the list" even if they were super busy.

If you can't find someone via your network, then you will need to reach out to other sources. Upwork.com and Guru.com are great places to find contractors for all kinds of online skill sets and projects. There are also some amazing online directories for specific types of professionals that can easily be found online.

Being that you aren't hiring a full-time employee, I wouldn't look towards the traditional strategies of posting a job ad in newspapers or via online job boards. Not only is that an expensive option, chances are that you will not attract contractors as most people who peruse job ads are looking for full time employment.

SIDENOTE

The current buzz online is all about how to use social media to market your business and find new clients. Not only are social media tools great for marketing, they can also be a highly effective way to source team members.

You could post your project request on Facebook, Twitter, or send a targeted message to your LinkedIn community. Part of what is so great about these social networks is that not only are you reaching YOUR friends, but with the six degrees of separation you're also reaching friends of friends who might be a great fit for your needs.

3. Hiring

I've found that unless you are hiring a core team member, you don't need to do a traditional interview route with most contractors. What you do need to do is ensure that they have the skills you are looking for.

Ask to see their website, portfolio, and examples of projects similar to yours. If you are hiring someone for a big project, such as a website redesign, you may want to ask them for references where they've done similar work. Keep it simple, other online business owners won't have the time to answer a lot of reference questions for you. I would simply just ask the person how it was to work with the contractor, and if they have any tips for doing so. You may just get a few "they are great!" responses, which in my mind counts as a good reference.

Check on the contractor's availability and timelines – how long will it take them to finish your project? What is their current workload? When can they start? If they are super busy they may not be able to start for a month and you may need something in a week.

What are their rates and how do they want to be paid? We prefer to pay people via PayPal, and some international contractors don't like to use PayPal. This is something to discuss upfront as this can cause an issue later if payment options are limited.

Once you've found a match, the hiring process is usually as simple as getting started! I generally don't worry too much about formal agreements unless we are hiring a core team member. If someone is just going to be editing an audio file for you, it seems a bit much to ask them to sign an agreement upfront. In most cases, it's enough to send an email outlining what you discussed about the project, such as the deliverables from them, the timeline for completion and the budget. Ask them to reply to the email and voilà! You have a basic agreement in place. For example, I would send an email that says:

Hi Beth,

I just wanted to follow up with an email to confirm what we talked about today.

As discussed, I am looking for a custom illustrated banner for my new website. I'm looking for the banner to be 800 pixels wide and no taller than 200 pixels. I'd like the illustration to be of me on my computer and my girls around me. I've attached a picture of us that you can use as a reference. I really like this banner at examplewebsite.com as an example. [It's nice to include an example for them to work from where possible.]

I'm looking to have a draft by next Wednesday, and will need the final done by Friday, which you confirmed works on your end. The cost for the banner will be $100, *which includes one revision and final copy, to be paid to you via PayPal on completion of banner.*

Will you please let me know if I've missed anything? If this looks good, just pop me a quick note to say 'great' and we are ready to roll. Thanks!

Or, if you have been going back and forth via email to discuss the project, those emails will also suffice as an agreement. Just be sure to keep a copy of them in case you ever need to refer back to confirm rates, etc.

Before hiring a core team member, I recommend trying them out on a single project or two first, to ensure that there is a fit for the role (you never really know until they get to work). When you are ready to bring them onto the team long-term, have them sign a Contractors Agreement outlining their role, responsibilities, termination notice, status as a contractor, etc. If you don't already have a Contractors Agreement, you can find some great resources online to craft one specific to your needs and where you live.

4. Training

Depending on the role, you may need to train a person on the various systems and tools that you use. Being that you've already created an SOP (as discussed in the last chapter) this will streamline the training process as it gives new team members a place to turn to for a 'how-to' reference. It is also a great way for you to see where the gaps are in your SOP, as you will find yourself saying, "Here's how to do this ... ooops, that's not in there yet," or responding to questions that highlight what's missing. So you can update the SOP along the way.

I've found that it is still best to take a bit of time to walk a person through their role, responsibilities and the bigger picture of the business. If you just say, "Here's the SOP, go to work!" it generally doesn't give them enough of a foundation to work from. Take the time to schedule a phone call, give them a tour of your client's websites and backend systems and show them where to find the information they need in the SOP. If you give people the big picture it gives them something bigger to plug into, which I've found to be so important in the long run. If your team members get what is going on from a bigger perspective, they will be able to contribute in larger ways down the road.

SIDENOTE

Skills Not Required. Be open to the idea of hiring someone who may not yet have all the skills you need. When I worked for a local placement company in Calgary (before I worked online) we used to say, "Hire for personality, not for skills." Anyone can learn a skill, but personality and fit can not be taught.

This means, of course, that you may have to spend more time and effort in training someone. In our experience we've found that the people that we've trained from scratch almost always work out better than those we hired based on skills only. In some cases, a person who comes with 'skills intact' may be already set in their way of doing things and have to unlearn it. This is way more work in the long run than just training them fresh.

There are always exceptions to the rule of course, and if you can find someone who is a great fit and already has the skills, well, that is ideal! Just don't discount someone who doesn't know your systems if you notice that they "click" well with you and the business. A little investment in training this person could pay dividends in the long run.

Me and my shadow

One of our favorite training methodologies is shadowing – have the person follow you around virtually so they can learn in "real time." This is very easy to do online, simply blind carbon copy (Bcc) the trainee on various emails or tasks in your project manager that apply to what they need to learn and follow up as needed to explain things in greater detail.

This is highly effective for a couple of reasons. First, it keeps training from becoming a new task in your already busy schedule. Instead, you can train the person within the natural flow of the business. As various situations come up, shadow them on the process and send them extra instructions or details as needed.

Secondly, people are much more likely to remember something when they see it "live and in-action" versus hear about it in theory. When you try to teach everything up front, chances are that most of the information won't stick as they haven't had a chance to apply it. Whereas when you teach via shadowing, the trainee gets to see real examples of the situations and will retain the information at a much higher level.

Don't forget to assign your trainee the task of updating the SOP along the way with the various things they are learning.

5. Managing

In our project management chapter, we talked about managing as it applies to "getting stuff done." As the OBM a key part of your role is to make sure the right things get done in the right way, at the right time and by the right people. This is what good management is all about.

Alongside that day to day management of the team and their tasks, I also really love to work with team members on their own growth and expansion. Apply your coaching approach and get to know them at a deeper level. What are the goals of those who are on your team? How can you help them work towards those goals and give them some experience to get there? For example, your VA may have a real interest in WordPress and web design. Perhaps they could work on creating a new template for your client's blog the next time it needs a bit of freshening up?

For me, there is nothing more rewarding than seeing a fellow team member grow into a new specialty or focus for their own business. This may mean that they stop working for you in order to focus on this new area of their business.

We have always considered the VA role to be a place to come and grow versus to come and stay. On average, our VAs stay with us for about two to three years and then they move onto bigger and better things either within or outside of the business. Human beings are meant to grow and expand, in both work and in life. If you really get this and come to expect this from your team members, then it doesn't have to be a bad thing when someone moves on. It becomes a graduation of sorts, something to celebrate, and chances are they can remain a part of your team with their new focus.

One of my clients used to say that one of her definitions of success in business is how many contractors go on to become so huge she would never want to have to afford them.

The OBM is also responsible for taking care of any challenges that come up within the team. Perhaps someone is late with their projects, or keeps making mistakes, or maybe two team members are not getting along for some reason. The key here is to simply treat people with respect and have an honest conversation about it. Open a dialogue and find out what's up. Something may be going on in their personal life that is causing them stress. Or they may be getting so busy in their own business that they are having a hard time keeping up.

Then, give them the chance to suggest how they would like to fix the situation; put the ball in their court. People are much more likely to stick to a solution that they created themselves than a solution that is imposed upon them. If they are simply so busy in their business that they can't keep up perhaps it is time for them to let go of some of the work they are doing for you and pass it along to someone else? This gives them the opportunity to choose the work they enjoy doing and let go of the stuff they don't like quite as much, which is something that team members earn along the way.

Understand too that everyone makes mistakes – unless you start to see a pattern of mistakes it probably isn't cause for any kind of intervention. Part of the beauty of working online is that everything is fixable. Compared to offline mistakes (e.g., putting the wrong address on a printed flyer) you can fix most online mistakes quickly and easily. If someone setup the wrong price for a product in the shopping cart, fix it and contact anyone it may apply to. If there is an error on a webpage this can be easily corrected. Or maybe a broadcast is sent out with the wrong link in it – just resend the broadcast with an apology and the correct link.

There seems to be a rite of passage in working online – what I call the First Big Mistake. Every VA that I've ever worked with has had this happen, myself included!

Sarah Noked recalls her First Big Mistake with a new client:

> I remember when I started to work with a new client and was tasked with contacting GoDaddy to consolidate some of her hosting plans. She had a number of websites and wanted to consolidate some of the websites under one cPanel. I thought, easy! While I was on support with GoDaddy, the support technician walked me through the steps of cancelling one of her cPanels. Immediately following that innocent click I realized I had single handedly wiped out my client's entire website. We had NO BACKUP!

I felt my heart sink and was so upset. I immediately told my new client and assured her I would put things back in order. However, since this was a new client I wasn't even entirely sure how I would do it. Lucky for me I could locate some screenshots of her site via the website www.waybackmachine.org and together with my very talented developer we put back the site. Piece by piece. You'd better believe I check twice before I ever update any client's website in any way without a backup these days!

The beauty of a big mistake is that it makes us much more careful about the work we are doing, because we don't want to repeat it again!

Stepping into an existing team

Quite often you will be joining a team that is already working with the client (and in some cases has been around a very long time). You may be familiar with some of the team members already, especially if you have done a 'dating' project or two with the client (which we do recommend before taking on the OBM role, and we'll talk more about that later). There is a bit of an art to joining an already established team, so here are a few tips:

- Understand how the other team members are feeling. You are essentially a stranger who is coming in to play a pretty key role in the business. It is natural for people to be a bit suspicious or unsure of you until they get to know you. It is your responsibility to tread lightly in the beginning and give people an opportunity to get to know, like and trust you. Be authentic and don't try to "play a role."

The role of an OBM may be quite new to them (if your client hasn't had an OBM before), and they may not be used to what it is that you are doing in the business. They may be used to going directly to your client for everything, and it may take some time to create and establish new channels of communication in the team. In some instances they are quite happy to have another person to go to, as the client may have been too busy or not quite sure how to handle certain situations. Suggesting they read a copy of this book can help too.

- Ask them to co-create with you. Your role as the OBM is to *coordinate* the growth of the business, not to *take over*. Make it very clear that you want and need their input, especially as it applies to streamlining and simplifying business systems and processes. An existing team is a goldmine of ideas for how to fix and improve things.

- Get to know them. What are their own personal goals for their business? What else would they love to try and grow into within the business? What do they do for fun outside of work? When you make a personal connection with someone it can make working together a more enjoyable experience

Building up your own delegation habit

After working with Sage Lavine for 4 years, Certified OBM® Jenn Sebastian made the transition from being Sage's VA to becoming her Business and Operations Manager. Jenn now manages a team of 15 people for this multi-million dollar business. There have certainly been challenges along the way, however the biggest challenge for Jenn has been breaking the habit of "doing" versus "managing."

As Jenn says "I was always the doer and moving to managing a team that 'does the work' instead required me to build my leadership and delegation skills. My focus is to ensure each person not only understands what they're doing and why, but also feels excited about their work and empowered to own their part in the success of a project. It's tough in the beginning to make this transition as it always takes longer to train people on a task than it is to just do it myself in the moment, however it has paid off in the long run by freeing me up to focus on the big picture and partner with Sage on creating the direction of the business."

Perhaps you can relate to what Jenn is sharing. Many OBMs have been the one doing the work at some point – which is a great way to learn and get the experience we need to play the OBM role. So our natural inclination is to do the work ourselves, usually without giving it a second thought.

However as your client's business grows (which it surely will, with your help), it is simply impossible for you to be both doer and manager. Even if it doesn't seem necessary right now, I invite you to start working on your delegation muscle. And let your clients know, so they can be paying you to do what you do best – manage. You'll hire others, at a lesser rate, for the "doing."

CHAPTER 8

LOOKING AT THE NUMBERS - MONEY MANAGEMENT

*Clients want someone who can help them
keep an eye on the bottom line*

I remember one of my professors in my last semester of college asking us, "What is the definition of a business?"

Being students, we came up with some lengthy and in-depth descriptions. The answer itself was surprisingly simple.

A business makes a profit.

If you aren't making a profit (or working towards making a profit) than you don't have a business, you have a hobby. (And it's truly surprising how many businesses are really hobbies, but that is a whole other topic.)

I always find it funny that business owners want to make money, but many of them seem almost allergic to managing their money. They may be very good at bringing in revenue and may in fact have a consistent six- or seven-figure income. But ask them any specifics about their profit or expenses and they just shake their heads and assume that since money is coming in they must be doing OK. Outside of getting a yearly income statement from their accountant, many business owners don't keep proper track of what is going on with their money on a regular basis.

Is their business really making money? Is their income larger than their expenses? You hear about people who win millions in the lottery and end up penniless within years. Well, sadly there are a surprising number of businesses that can tell a similar story – they may have high revenues but not have much money in the bank at the end of the day.

Making money is not the name of the game – profit is the name of the game. To earn a profit, you need to make more than you spend. If you want to make more money, there are only two ways to do it: increase your income or decrease your expenses.

It is vital for any business to keep track of their numbers on a regular basis to know if they're making a profit. I'm not talking about being an accountant here, what I'm talking about is common sense money management. And as an OBM, you can help by collecting the information the client needs to truly see what is going on in their business. With this information in hand they can measure their success (or lack thereof) in various areas of their business, make changes, try new things and see how those changes affect the numbers that count.

What should you track? Let's break it down.

Web statistics

Being an online-based business, your client's website is usually the hub of their business activity, and traffic plus conversion is the magic formula of growing a business online. Track how many people are visiting your client's websites, and of those visitors how many are taking action (e.g., opting into the list or making a purchase).

With this information you can see exactly where your client's business can be improved. If they have decent traffic but aren't making any sales, you need to focus on conversion. If there isn't much traffic coming to the websites, look at ways to boost traffic. As you continually work towards improving your clients' websites (as you should), you will be able to see improvement in the numbers, as well.

A good web statistics program such as Google Analytics will give you all the information you need. This is something to track on a monthly basis (or weekly if your client has a lot of traffic, say 1,000 visitors or more in a day).

The list

In the online world your client's list is King. Every online business should have a list of targeted (interested) people with whom they keep in touch on a regular basis. This is a very important part of relationship-based selling and long-term sustainability. Clients will usually have a main list (usually called an email or newsletter list) and potential sub-lists of prospects, clients and affiliates.

You want to keep track of the number of people on your client's various lists. Also, track how many people join each week and each month. When you see a surge in subscriptions, what caused it? How can you replicate that again?

For example, we once saw a surge of signups to a client's list, and with a bit of digging we found out that a JV partner had recently done a big promotion for their own product and we were getting exposure on their Thank You page. That led us to look for similar people we could swap Thank You page messages with.

Sales/Revenue

List each product, service and offering that your client sells, and anything else that brings money into the business. Then keep track of the amounts sold for each item on a weekly or monthly basis.

What is selling or not selling? Of those items that are selling, how can you continue to improve sales? Of those that aren't selling, how can you increase sales or perhaps look at letting that item go? (Just because something is for sale doesn't mean you have to sell it forever.)

Launches & Promotions

Whenever you do a launch or a promotion you want to track the results. Tracking links are great for this – you can set up a tracking link via the shopping cart system and monitor the number of clicks and sales from that specific promotion. You'll know if you've made a profit if the resulting sales are more than the cost of implementing the promotion. Keep in mind here that your costs can be both direct (such as the cost of placing an ad on Facebook) or indirect (such as paying someone to manage your affiliate program).

If the promotion isn't making money you can either a) revise your approach and try again or b) scrap it all together and focus on other promotional strategies. I like to use the "three strikes and you're out" rule here – if you try something three times and it doesn't create a profit, move on. There are lots of promotional opportunities out there, so don't get attached to something if it isn't making you money. Likewise, just because something works for someone else, that doesn't necessarily mean it will work for your client. Every business is different and will have its own best way to market and promote.

Expenses

How much money is the business spending on systems, tools and team members each month? I find this to be a particularly common area for improvement in a client's business. Chances are, your client may not have a clue about their total expenses and may be surprised (and possibly frightened) by the number.

What are the current expenses and where or how can you cut back on those expenses? I tend to err on the side of being miserly (dare I say cheap?) when it comes to systems. Why spend hundreds of dollars a month on a system that is either a) not being used or b) could be combined into another system? For example, if your client has a separate autoresponder system, affiliate system, ad tracking system and shopping cart, suggest they combine it all into an all-in-one shopping cart.

Also, how much is your client spending on team members each month? Is it necessary to have everyone on the payroll each and every month? Is each team member "paying their way" in terms of how much their work is contributing to the bottom line? Is your client paying a higher rate than necessary for certain things? Are they paying a specialist to do something that their VA could do for less? I see this happen a lot, e.g., paying a webmaster $75 per hour to send an email broadcast instead of assigning that task to the VA for $35 per hour.

In an information-based business, you generally **don't want your team expenses to be more than 20% of total revenue.** If expenses are more than this then your client may need to take a good look at how they are doing business and where their money is being spent. We've found that with a few tweaks, a business owner can usually make a substantial decrease to expenses to increase their profits overall.

And if you can help them do that, you better believe they will be singing praises to their OBM!

Talking dollars and sense

Even though a lot of business owners may not be 100% aware of their numbers, if you speak to them in terms of dollars they will certainly sit up and take notice.

So anytime your client is considering a new idea or strategy, be sure to "bring it home" as far as how it will affect the bottom line. For example, say your client is launching a new membership program and needs to setup a system to manage the back-end. They come to you and say, "Hey, Bob is using this great system called MemberGate – let's use that one for our new membership."

You investigate and realize that MemberGate costs $4,995 or more depending on your needs. As the OBM we always want to see if there is a more cost-effective solution out there, so we do a bit of research and see what other business owners are using for their memberships. In talking to a few of our colleagues we discover that many of them are using LearnDash, which only costs $199. Combined with a customized WordPress blog as the "member resource area," your total costs in setting up this solution could be as low as $2,000.

That's a potential savings of $3,000 for your client.

Now, keep in mind that when you approach your client with these different options, you need to be able to adequately compare the two systems beyond just the initial cost difference. For example, not only is LearnDash less expensive, but you can customize it, while with MemberGate you are stuck using their templates. Also, with LearnDash you can grow to an unlimited number of members for the same low price, whereas with MemberGate once you reach 1,000 members you will need to spend more to upgrade to the next level.

To just say to your client "LearnDash looks like a great solution and it's cheaper, maybe we should go with that one," isn't enough. If you approach it in a slightly different way it can have a much bigger impact. I would say to my client "Here are the two options, which have a difference of $34,000 in upfront costs. Based on your membership model of charging $27 per month per member, with MemberGate you won't see a profit until after 185 subscriptions, whereas with the LearnDash system you will be able to enjoy a profit after just 75 subscriptions."

Because it's not just about the cost – it's about overall profit and how quickly they can reach that point. When you bring it back to that bottom line for your clients they will be able to make the best decision possible and enjoy more profits with less effort.

As a side benefit, you are also training your clients to start to think about profit in their business. Again, many business owners tend to look at revenue only and really aren't giving profit the proper consideration. You're helping them to connect the dots – they come to understand that, "When I do X, it means Y to my bottom line." This additional benefit to having an OBM on the team can really help a business owner start to focus their energy and attention where it counts – the balance in their bank account at the end of the day.

CHAPTER 9

LIVING THE DREAM - MAKING MORE WHILE WORKING LESS

You know you want to!

The standard business model of a service-based professional is the exchange of time for money. You work a certain amount of time, and you are paid an hourly wage for that time. Almost everyone I've talked to in the industry works this way, including the many OBMs that I interviewed while writing this book. The thing is that there are only so many hours in a day, and only a certain number of those that you can work.

Say that you have decided that you have 20 hours a week available to work in and on your business, to keep the balance of your time for your family as well as time for yourself.

Of those 20 hours, it's likely that 15 are billable hours – you'll need the rest of the time for administrative and marketing activities.

If you are charging your clients $35 per hour as a virtual assistant and you are working 15 billable hours a week, that equals $525 per week or $2,100 per month. If you plan on taking off four weeks of vacation per year, this works out to be $25,200 of revenue from your business for the year.

$25,000 a year is a good income for working part-time hours and enjoying the flexibility that a virtually based business allows, however that is the limit that you can make under this model of exchanging time for money. If you want to work a maximum of 20 hours a week at $35 per hour you will make $25K and no more.

What if you want to make more money in your business?

How would you like to make $60,000 a year? At $35 per hour that would require that you work about 40 hours a week (given that 5-ish hours a week are non-billable). You could certainly work these extra hours; however I'm guessing that you started your home-based business for a reason and that adding more hours that would take you away from your family may not be feasible for you.

The time-for-money model puts a limit on the success of your business – not only from a monetary perspective, but also from a satisfaction and growth perspective.

How can I make more money while working the same (or less) hours?

Would you like to be able to have unlimited growth opportunity in your online support business, even if you are already at the bursting point? What if you could make more money while working the same or less hours? If this sounds attractive to you, then read on!

There are a few options that will allow you the freedom to increase your income without adding to your workload.

Option 1: Raise your hourly rates

There are two ways to increase your rates and making more money per hour: you can start charging more for the "regular" VA work that you do, or you can start doing "specialty" work that you can charge a higher rate for.

Regular VA skills

These are the foundational skills that business owners are looking for in a virtual assistant, and for which you would charge your regular rates.

- Shopping cart administration
- Email broadcasting
- Basic website maintenance
- Autoresponder Setup
- Blog / social media posting

- Affiliate administration
- Customer service
- Word processing / Typing
- Email management
- Creating PDF documents
- Online research
- PowerPoint presentations
- Database management

Specialty skills

These are specialty skills that most clients need on a project basis, and for which you will want to charge your higher rates.

- Website design
- Graphic design
- Writing / Editing
- Transcription
- Copywriting
- Audio / Video editing
- Blog Design / customization
- Bookkeeping
- Event management
- Project management
- Social media management

- Internet marketing strategy
- Search engine marketing
- Joint venture sourcing and management
- Online business management

At the time of writing, the industry standard for regular VA services is in the $25-$45 per hour range. How do you know where to set your rates within that range? It depends on both your experience and your clientele. Generally, VAs charge on the lesser end if they are just getting started or are still developing the full set of skills that they would like to offer. Once you have more experience you can raise your hourly rate accordingly.

Clients in certain industries may pay less than others, so get to know what the standard rates are for the clients you are working with. Having worked with coaches and consultants over the years, I've found that most of them are looking to pay in the $30-$40 per hour range for a VA and they really don't want to pay more than that if they can help it. Keep in mind that if most people are charging say $25 per hour to serve your target market and you suddenly raise your rates to $40 per hour this may affect how often you are hired in comparison to your fellow VAs.

You may be thinking, "Hey, I know my skills are worth more than the standard rates," and you would like to charge a higher hourly rate. Be prepared to answer the question:

Why should I pay you $50 an hour when I can hire your fellow VA for $30 an hour?

If you are offering a specialized service of any kind this will certainly justify a higher hourly rate (usually in the $50-$100+ per hour range). A specialized service is something that requires a level of special training, such as web design or graphic design.

Of course, being an OBM falls into the range of specialty skills, as you are providing a higher level of service to your clients.

> *I remember a conversation years ago with Amy Maeder of DesignFormare.com about raising rates. Amy had been working as a VA for a year or so, in conjunction with the web and graphic design business that she'd already had for years. She was at the 'bursting point' in her business and decided that she really needed to shift her focus to some higher paying work. Her lower-paying VA work had her so busy that she was having to say no to some higher-paying design projects that had come across her plate. In her own words:*

> *"I could work 15 hours a day at my VA rate or work 8 hours a day at my design rate, and still make the same amount of money. It's time for me to make some changes."*

Charging a higher rate for specialized services is a great example of how to escape the bursting zone without losing any income.

Option #2: Hire your own team

Hire other VAs and support professionals to work as part of your team, so you can take on more business and not have to do all the work yourself. More and more virtual assistants are taking this route once they hit the bursting point. Rather than turn away clients, they hire their own team of VAs and create an agency business.

The plus side of this option is that it allows a VA to truly become a scalable, growth-oriented business. The have the option to grow their business (and income) as much as they want, depending on how many people they have on their team. You can continue to charge what you've been charging and pay a percentage of that rate to the VAs on your team.

A few considerations if you decide to go this route:

- As you grow your team your role becomes less of a 'doer' and more of a manager of everything that is going on – you essentially become your own OBM! Some people find this to be a bit of a challenge, especially if they enjoy working directly with clients.

- You are responsible for the work that your team members are doing, and as such you need to set up systems and training to ensure they are delivering quality work. This requires working quite closely with team members, more closely than you may think. It's easy to assume that people will provide the same level of service and do things the way you would, whereas they may need a lot of training and leadership to do so (especially at the beginning). Stay plugged into your team members and what they are doing.

- There are no guarantees with people – someone on your team may have to quit suddenly for whatever reason, which could leave you scrambling to complete the work that they are responsible for. I've seen it happen time and again, both in my previous life as a corporate recruiter and as an online business manager. You think you have the perfect team than BAM! Someone quits or makes a big mistake and you are left with a mess to fix. Just know that this will happen at some point. It's not a matter of IF it's a matter of WHEN. The key is to be prepared and calm in the moment, and to look for immediate solutions and replacements so that your clients still receive the level of service they require.

- Some clients may really want to work with you directly and may not want to work with other members of your team. This is especially common when you started with them as a "team of one" and then began growing your business along the way. On the flip side, other clients really like the fact that they are hiring a team so that they have more than one person to rely on.

- You need to have very strong time tracking and project management systems in place with a team. Who is working on what for which clients? You need to be able to answer that question at a glance. Plus, you are responsible for billing for all the work done each month, which in itself can become a huge task.

If you are going to build your own VA agency you will essentially become a business in your own right – complete with all the challenges (headaches!) and rewards (money!) of owning a growth-based business. It comes down to personal choice, knowing the differences between working solo versus creating your own team.

As an OBM, you can work with your own team or as a solo. There are OBMs who bring a team with them, providing the "full meal deal" agency experience for their clients. Other OBMs work with a client's existing team members and/or hire other team members to work direct with the client.

From a day-to-day perspective the work you are doing with the team will look the same – you are responsible for managing the team members, ensuring that things get done in a timely manner with a focus on generating revenue. Working solo is ideal for the client who doesn't want to have all their eggs in one basket. I'm a big fan of "spreading the risk" for business owners. If everyone who works with them is part of a single company, what happens if that company can no longer work with that business owner (they quit, have a falling out with the owner, etc.)? This leaves the business owner without ANYONE on their team, which in my mind is a very scary situation. Compare that to having several independent contractors that work directly for the client; as team members come and go (which they always will), the business owner still has other members of the team to fill in and keep things afloat while replacements are found.

Again, it comes down to the business owner's preference. Some people really like having that "full meal deal" solution, and don't mind having the risk of all eggs in one basket. Whereas other business owners are fine with (and may prefer) having a team of independent contractors supporting their business.

Option #3: Working on incentive

I am such a HUGE fan of this option as it opens up so many doors to grow your business and income.

Incentive-based pay means that you get paid a percentage of the revenue or profit that your clients make, be it on individual projects or on their business income as a whole.

This is the icing on the cake when it comes to working as an OBM, and in my humble opinion it should be the goal of any OBM-client relationship for a few reasons:

- The sky is the limit when it comes to potential earnings – as your client's business grows (as it will, with your help) your income will grow alongside.

- You are truly invested in the success of your client's business because the more they make the more you make. When you are paid hourly, you will make the same amount of money regardless of how well your client's business is doing. This is not to say that you don't care about your client's success if you are working hourly – it is important regardless– but being paid on incentive brings it to a whole new level.

- There is a much higher level of satisfaction in this working arrangement, knowing that you will benefit alongside your client as you help them grow their business. It can be a tough pill to swallow (even on a subconscious level) to be working so hard and see your client's business grow by leaps and bounds and still get paid the same amount as you were at the beginning. Even raising your hourly rates still leaves your income capped.

The heart of the OBM-client partnership is in sharing the growth of the business, both energetically and financially. This is the opportunity that every OBM has as it really is the full expression of a successful partnership on both sides. The client has someone that is truly plugged into the success of their business (which is what every business owner wants) and the OBM is being rewarded for their commitment in a bigger way. Now that's a recipe for a long-term successful partnership!

What does an incentive-based pay structure look like?

As an OBM you need to be paid a base retainer or "draw against commission" amount plus a percentage-based incentive.

BASE + INCENTIVE = OBM INCOME

I generally recommend that you choose a flat rate for a span of hours as your base pay. For example, you could have a flat rate of $1,500/month which covers working 25-ish hours in a month. You can loosely base this amount on your hourly rate multiplied by the expected number of hours you will work in a month. Some months you may work a bit more than the 25-ish hour range, other months it may be less. In my experience this all evens out in the end (and is irrelevant anyhow as you are really being paid on incentive).

Sidenote: There is no such thing as working on commission ONLY as an OBM. There are lot of business owners out there who think that incentive-based payment should mean that there is no base and you get paid strictly on commission only. It makes sense in theory, but it simply doesn't work.

As I've explained to business owners many times, for someone to be willing to invest time and energy in their company they need to know that they are being paid at least a base payment of some kind. It can take a while for incentive-based payment to really kick in, which means that someone could be expected to work for free for weeks or months before they ever make a dime. Like anyone else, VAs and OBMs need to make a living, and will go where the money is. Even if there is the potential to make oodles of money down the road, they need to pay bills now.

Besides, most business owners who want someone to work commission only are usually asking for that because they aren't making money yet in their business and can't afford to pay someone. If that is the case, they aren't ready to hire an OBM yet anyways (or anyone for that matter). A business owner who is ready for and understands the importance of hiring an OBM will gladly pay a base as part of your incentive package.

The incentive comes from an agreed upon percentage of revenue from either a) one or more business lines or b) their business income as a whole. This can vary depending on how you are working with the client. You may be paid a percentage of their programs, events and product sales, because those are the areas where you're providing support, but nothing from their individual coaching income, because you're not involved in that aspect of the business. It all depends on how your work is affecting the bottom line.

The incentive also kicks in when you help a client reach a certain revenue milestone. For example, before you came along your client was making $15K a month from their membership program. Being that an OBM's job is to help the client grow their business, your incentive-based pay could kick in when their revenue hits $20K a month, something they couldn't have done without your help. Makes sense, right?

Percentage-wise you are generally looking at anywhere from 5% to 10% of revenue, again depending on what the client is doing. This needs to be based on the client's business model and associated expenses. For example, they may run a monthly coaching program and need to pay their associate coaches a percentage of the revenue. In that case, you may be looking at the lower range. However, they may also be selling online training programs that have less overhead costs, and therefore your share could be in the higher range. You could have a mix of incentives for each different revenue stream with the same client.

I also highly recommend that the incentive be based on revenue and not profit.

To base payment on profit is simply a headache – to figure out what you are paid each month you will need to wait for all expenses to come in, allocate them to each revenue stream and then determine what you should be paid. Then there is always the complication of expenses that could be applied equally to one or more revenue streams – it can quickly get very complicated!

If you are paid on revenue it is a straightforward calculation – we made $X in sales this month so I get 10%, done!

In my experience it is cleaner and simpler to base incentive off revenue versus profit. Some clients may not want to go that route, in which case it is fine to base it on profit. Just note that the percentage amounts will need to be higher.

Breaking the hourly habit

Some people are scared of incentive-based pay. Why? It means that you have to think about your income in a totally different way.

Instead of knowing that you will be paid $X for the time work each month, you are taking the risk that your income could fluctuate. You could end up working a whole bunch of hours just to get a base amount each month! If you'd worked the same number of hours for an hourly rate you would be paid more.

Breaking the hourly habit is about accepting the uncertainty of incentive-based pay. Yes, there is the risk of working more hours than you're paid for. The flip side, of course, is that you could also end up making more (MUCH more, in the long run) than you would hourly.

There is no guarantee either way, which is part of the risk, and I know some OBMs who simply aren't willing to go that route. They prefer the assurance of knowing that if they work 35 hours this month that is what they'll be paid for. There's nothing wrong with this, it just comes down to personal choice based on your tolerance for risk.

Working on incentive also requires that you step it up and play a bigger game. You are taking on a level of responsibility that simply is not there with an hourly payment structure. Being paid on incentive puts you in the spotlight, so that if revenue targets aren't achieved you have to answer to that. This can be quite intimidating for some, although I'm a big fan of stepping into the fear and going for it anyways. It really gives you an opportunity to stretch in ways you may not have considered before, and to enjoy the ride of seeing a business grow, stumble and thrive (one of the best rides out there!).

Personally, I hated getting paid on an hourly basis; partially because I hated having to "punch a clock" (flashback to my corporate days!) but mostly because I don't think the value of my service comes from how much time I spent doing something. It comes from how what I'm doing is going to affect the client's business. If I spent five hours setting up an online customer help desk, which in turn saves my clients countless hours of admin time in responses along with lost revenue due to missed emails, what is that really worth? Is it worth five hours at my hourly rate? Or is it worth what it saves my client on the bottom line?

CHAPTER 10

THE GOOD, THE BAD AND THE (NOT SO) UGLY – REAL LIFE AS AN OBM

Know Thyself

Before you dive into becoming an OBM for your current or future clients, I'd like to take a moment for you to review all the benefits and pitfalls of working at this level.

Having worked as an OBM for eight years before I started training Certified OBMs back in 2009, I'm rather partial to playing this bigger role for clients. However, I also know some people who have dipped their toe in the water of working as an OBM (and in some cases jumped right into the pool) only to find that it wasn't for them. This resulted in some big stress and broken relationships as the OBM struggled to deliver what they promised to their clients.

I invite you to take a good, honest look at yourself in the mirror here, and I daresay that by the end of the chapter you will either feel a) excited about becoming an OBM or b) not inspired at all by the idea. (Remember, fear can be a good thing, so if you are afraid that could be a sign that you are ready to shift into this bigger role!)

Why it's great to be an OBM

Significant earning potential

As we discussed in the last chapter, working as an OBM offers the opportunity to make significantly more money than you would in a traditional VA or online support role. Getting out of the mindset of being paid money in exchange for time and shifting to an incentive-based pay system literally blows the roof off any income limitations.

By way of example, with one of my clients I was working on average about 25 hours a month (some months less, some months a bit more). She offered a series of 6-month coaching programs which became very popular in her niche market. As a result, I was making anywhere from $2,000-$5,000 a month as part of my incentive plan. That works out to be over $100 per hour for the 25-ish hours I was working in a month – well worth my effort, yes? Imagine having two or three clients that you work with at this level – that could be a very lucrative living for working part-time from the comfort of home.

This didn't happen overnight; we had worked together for a couple of years before her business reached this level of income. Just know that it is possible when you work with the right client (which we'll talk about in the next chapter).

Work with a select few clients

Working as an OBM allows you to work more closely with fewer clients (generally two or three), compared to the traditional VA model of having lots of clients with varying needs and time commitments.

I love to use this analogy when it comes to client load: imagine that you are literally carrying around each client on your back. It doesn't matter if you do one hour a month for them or 40 hours a month, they each weigh the same amount. This can get heavy if you have a lot of clients!! And darn tiring, as well.

Energetically there is a truth to this scenario. You are "carrying around" each client that you are engaged with. This is a huge cause of the bursting point that we talked about earlier, as an hourly based model (which we are getting away from yes?) requires that we fill those hours with work to make a living. And for most online support professionals this means having a lot of clients, quite often 10 or more, each of whom has different needs and deadlines.

I'm sure you've had those days when it seems like every client you have pops up demanding your services – very stressful! It can literally be a brain scrambler trying to keep track of what needs to be done for each client, not to mention how you will find the time to do all that work.

When playing a bigger role with your client in an OBM capacity, you have less people to "carry around" on your back. You have two or three clients who may pop up all at once asking for help, instead of eight or ten. It's easier to focus your energy on each person, instead of feeling scattered and drained trying to keep track of it all.

Establishing yourself as an expert

When you help your clients create success, you will become considered an expert yourself in your client's niche market. When good things are happening the word gets around, and people will soon come to recognize you for the role you are playing in that success. And any good client will, of course, be gladly sharing how hiring an OBM has made all the difference for them and their business.

This kind of credibility can open new doors for you, bringing you different opportunities that you may never have considered before. You may be approached to do consulting with business owners to help them strategize and plan for growth, or to help train their team members on various systems and strategies. Any of these options will pay a nice hourly rate and don't have to take too much time in an already busy schedule.

Finding new clients by word of mouth

I never had to market my OBM business at all, because every single client I worked with came to me by word of mouth. A business owner's dream, yes? This is the reality of working at this level – more and more business owners are eager to hire an OBM which puts you in high demand.

When you have helped grow your client's business, word gets around and other business owners will come knocking at your door. The world of online business is a very connected community, and once people learn what you can do for your clients you will find that most (if not all) of your business will come by referral.

OBM clients are long(er) term clients

Being that you play a bigger role in your client's business, chances are that you will work with your OBM clients for a very long time. In our experience, most VAs have a core group of clients that they stay with long term (maybe 25%-50% of their hours) and outside of that they have several clients who come and go for various reasons. This means that they are constantly having to market themselves (which takes some effort) not to mention they have that energetic "hump" of starting to work with a new client. It takes time to get to know a new client before you really settle into a good working relationship.

That's not to say that OBM clients don't come and go. There are situations where they might make changes to their business and that can affect your role. I once had a client who had to move back to the UK, which of course affected the US-based coaching programs that he was running. He had to focus his efforts on his new location, which resulted in an end to our working relationship. On the flipside, I worked with one of my clients for well over seven years and our working relationship only ended because I started the Certified OBM® training program and decided to stop working with OBM clients directly.

You can really plug in to your client's business

There is a certain level of satisfaction that comes from working very closely with a client as their OBM. You get to celebrate the successes together with your clients, instead of just cheering them from the sidelines. You get to see your ideas and efforts come to life and enjoy the results of such.

This was always my favorite way to work with clients. I really loved getting to know their business, getting to know them and creating something bigger together than could ever be done alone. Isn't that the whole point of business? (Or life for that matter?)

Continuous learning and growth

I remember back in my corporate recruiting days when I was interviewing people daily who were looking for new jobs. When we asked them why they were looking for something new, nine times out of ten it was simply because they were bored. They had learned everything they could learn in their current position, and they weren't seeing any opportunity for growth with their current employer. Humans are meant to constantly evolve and change, and if they aren't challenged by new opportunities or situations in their work they will become dissatisfied very quickly.

This is what is so beautiful about working as an OBM – there is ALWAYS something new to learn, something to try that you haven't tried before. Bigger ways to stretch yourself, perhaps ways you didn't even consider to be possible in the past. I find that working for online-based businesses provides an extra level of learning compared to offline businesses. The Internet literally moves at the speed of light, new online systems, tools and strategies being created every day (every minute?) that can help grow your client's business. One can get seriously stuffed at this online business buffet!

Challenges of working as an OBM

There are aspects of this role that may provide a lot of stress for the OBM. It's really a matter of being prepared and knowing what you are getting into so that you can handle situations and not let them get the best of you.

Many People Still Don't Understand What an OBM Does

When the first edition of this book came out in 2008 many business owners had never heard of an OBM. 10 years later most people in the online world are familiar with the role of an OBM, but that doesn't mean they really understand what an OBM can do for them.

It not uncommon for a business owner to think of an OBM as something like a 'glorified VA' and not yet see the value of having someone who can run and grow the business with them.

I've also heard too many stories from business owners who worked with an untrained OBM that was delivering at the level of a VA – they were doing, not managing. They weren't happy with their experience and may be hesitant to hire an OBM again. This is a pet peeve of mine as it reflects poorly on the professional OBMs who are working hard to deliver at this level.

With the launch of the International Association of Online Business Managers in 2009 we standardized the OBM role and created an accepted set of responsibilities and expectations that the Certified OBM® brings to the table. With a clear definition of the OBM role you can set proper and achievable expectations with your clients from the start.

As an OBM you need to understand that not everyone knows what an OBM really does, and that you may need to educate them accordingly. This can be frustrating at times, but I consider it to be more of an opportunity not just for you as an OBM but for the Certified OBM industry at large.

When we educate and demonstrate to our clients what an OBM can do for them, we are playing a part in continuing to build a relatively new industry that will thrive for years to come.

Shouldering the responsibility

When working as an OBM you are taking on a higher level of responsibility than you would be in a traditional VA or online support role. This may be more than you are used to, and for some people can feel quite uncomfortable. As an OBM your responsibility increases in a few key ways:

- You are now responsible for helping to build a business, not just for getting stuff done.
- You are now responsible for ensuring that everyone on the team gets their work done (not always so easy to control!) and are no longer responsible for only what you do (which you can easily control).

- Your client is looking for you to help increase their bottom line, which needs to be considered in everything that you are doing.

This responsibility means that if something doesn't get done or doesn't provide an intended result, you have to answer to that. You need to be willing to look at a situation, acknowledge what went wrong, your role in that and how it can be fixed. This isn't a negative thing per se, rather it is a challenge that provides an opportunity for growth (usually for all concerned, not just you as OBM).

You need to know that this WILL happen; there will be times that things don't turn out the way that was planned. There will be times that the "you know what" hits the fan for whatever reason: targets may not be reached, contractors may suddenly go MIA in the middle of a launch or a website gets hacked. These things will happen, so the name of the game is not just to prevent them from happening but to be ready to handle them when they happen.

Business is a journey of course correction and continuation. There is no set path of success and each business has its own journey to get to their goals. It's a matter of trying something, seeing how it works, making improvements to the process and continuing. It is a matter of being willing to look objectively at what happened and how to fix it or do it differently next time around. There are times when emotions will flare, be it yours, the client's or other members of the team. As the OBM you want to be the calm in the center of the storm, working to diffuse any emotions and get everyone moving forward.

No room for mediocrity

At this level of responsibility you will continually be challenged, and you need to be willing to stretch yourself beyond what you are used to. This is a scary process for anyone – going somewhere new and different. The key is being willing to walk into that fear and not turn away from it. The key to getting over any fear is to simply face it. We've all had these experiences in our personal lives, and the same thing applies to business.

You simply cannot be mediocre when playing this bigger role with your clients. You need to be willing to step up and become more than who you were before. Working as an OBM is, in many ways, a journey of personal and professional growth. It is an excellent opportunity to exercise business muscles that you may not have used yet, knowing that you may be sore at first but that you will soon become much stronger for it.

Sometimes people aren't prepared to stretch, and it catches them off guard. I call this a "deer in the headlights" moment. I remember a time when I was at a recruitment training session and the facilitator called on me to role play a recruiting situation. I was caught totally off guard (I think I was daydreaming, to be honest) and my mind went blank – I couldn't think of a single thing to say! I literally sat there in silence, wishing the floor would open and swallow me whole. It was one of the most embarrassing moments in my working life.

The thing is that I wasn't prepared for or expecting to be stretched that day. I was ready to zone out for another boring training session. When I was asked to do a role play that was something new and uncomfortable for me, I froze. Not to say that this would never happen to me again (we all have our moments!) but I am now much more engaged in myself and willing to step it up when called upon by events or people in my life.

The risk of incentive-based payment

As already discussed, for some people the idea of incentive-based payment is quite frightening; the idea that they may work X hours and not make their hourly rate from that is a huge turnoff for them. They really want to know that they will work X and make X from that time spent.

If the idea of incentive-based payment is not an inspiration to you, then I would ask if you are ready to become an OBM. Being paid on incentive becomes a reflection of how well you are doing your job as an OBM. If you meet your goals you will be paid more than your base. If you don't meet your goals you won't be paid more, which means that something is off and needs to be looked at.

I remember trying to put one of our VAs on an incentive-based structure at one point, where she would start to play a bigger role in some projects (not an official OBM role, more like a "road to OBM" role) and get paid when we reached certain targets. She was willing to try, but then each month she would question the fact that she had worked X hours but only got paid a base which worked out to be less than her hourly rate. We discussed how this could be a temporary thing and that over time and with her continued engagement in the project there would come a tipping point where the incentive kicks in and she is being paid more than what her hourly rate would have been. She didn't like this and we ended up going back to paying her hourly. There is nothing wrong with this choice at all, it simply says to me that she wasn't ready or willing to work as an OBM and was better suited to working at the VA level.

Some people simply aren't ready or willing to take on the challenge of being an OBM. They aren't willing to up the ante and have the effectiveness of their work be reflected in their income. An OBM should be excited by the prospect of incentive-based pay, as it is the heart of what their job is – making more money for their clients and subsequently for themselves.

Having your eggs in fewer baskets

As already discussed, working as an OBM means working with fewer clients at a time – usually two or three clients. What happens if one of these clients goes away for some reason? They could have an unexpected change that comes up (such as the client who moved away) or you may decide to stop working with your client for some reason. Instead of losing maybe 10% of your income as would happen if you have 10 clients, you have now lost 30% to 50% of your income. Yipes!

This is certainly a concern for many people as they transition from VA to OBM. There is a certain safety buffer when you have lots of clients versus a few, and you need to be willing to take that leap and know that it will be fine. If you stop working with a certain client, there are many more business owners who are eager and ready to hire an OBM. Chances are you've probably had a number knock on your door already and can simply reach out to them.

Every OBM that I've talked to is now making more in their business with fewer clients, compared to when they were working as a VA. That's not to say there is a guarantee, just know that it is very common.

When life gets in the way

Take a good look at your life and ask yourself, "Do I have the time and energy to play a bigger game with my clients right now?" There may be times in your life when you don't have the time and energy available to be an OBM for your clients.

Perhaps you have young children, or even teenage children that need more of your attention. I also know of people who have had to put their businesses on hold to take care of an ailing parent. Or maybe you are dealing with a health issue that requires you to keep your life as stress free as possible.

When it comes to the reality of working as an OBM, the rule of thumb is to "know thyself." Be very upfront and honest with who you are, what you are willing to do (and not do) and decide from there. If the role of an OBM doesn't fit right now, put it aside and come back to it in a year or two. There is no expiry date on the opportunity, and as we've already seen over the past 10 years the demand for OBMs is continuing to grow exponentially as more clients realize the value of having one on their team.

CHAPTER 11

MAKING THE MATCH - YOUR IDEAL OBM CLIENT

Not all business owners are ready to hire an OBM
(even if they think they are).

We've spent this whole book talking about you – the OBM. There is an equally important partner in this process and that is the business owner – your (potential) client.

As much as you need to be ready to play this bigger role with your clients, THEY need to be equally ready in their business to hire an OBM.

How do you know if a client is ready to hire an OBM?

There are many business owners who are eager to hire an OBM, but not all of them are ready to do so, even if they think they are. Here are a few key things to look for when talking to a potential new client or considering whether your current clients are ready.

Clearly defined and proven business model

The role of the OBM is to help grow an existing business, so the business owner needs to have a firmly established and proven business model. They know who their target market is. They know exactly how they make their money – what are they selling, who is buying it and how all their products and services fit together.

If they are a brand-new business or are struggling, they aren't ready yet for an OBM. An OBM is an accelerant or catalyst that can create great results but needs a foundation to stand on. Asking a client who isn't already experiencing a modicum of success to take on an OBM can be like trying to fill up a glass of water with a fire hose – it's too much too soon. The business owner needs to get their business established first before they bring on an OBM.

Steady income

Hand-in-hand with having a proven business model is having a steady stream of income. In general, a business is ready to hire an OBM if they have at least a 6-figure annual income ($15K/month or more) that is steady and reliable throughout the year. If they make less or if their income is not yet reliable (lots of peaks and valleys) this can be an indicator that they don't have a strong proven business model and they may not be ready yet to hire an OBM.

Clear vision and goals

How passionate is the business owner about their business? Do they have a clear vision of what they want to achieve and a set path of how they are going to get there? This is the heart of any growing business and is NOT an area that can be delegated to an OBM.

Beware of the business owner who lacks enthusiasm and is just looking for someone to "take over" their business for them. It could be that they are burnt out, or perhaps just bored with their business. An OBM is there to help bring the business owners vision to life, not to create the vision for them.

> ### SIDENOTE
>
> I received this great question from a business owner:
>
> *Shouldn't [an OBM] be building their own business rather than building mine?*
>
> A good business manager doesn't necessarily want to build their own business. I like to look at business as the marriage of **vision (passion) + implementation**. A business manager is driven by implementation. They like to take an idea and bring it to life; they aren't necessarily the ones who like to come up with the ideas or vision themselves.

> Most business owners, on the other hand, are strong on the ideas or vision side of things but need help with implementation and management. I used to joke with a client of mine that I'm too busy "getting stuff done" to try and come up with ideas of my own! And as an OBM I liked it that way, as I found it very fulfilling to help my clients bring their own ideas and vision to life.
>
> Plus, if I am being paid on incentive then I am able to enjoy ongoing growth in my own income, similar to if it were my own business.

Likewise, a business owner could be passionate and excited about their business, but it may be something that isn't exciting to you at all. If you are working as a VA or other support professional, this scenario can be OK. However, if you are going to work as the client's OBM you absolutely NEED to be excited about what the client does. If it is boring to you, something you disagree with or if you have a moral issue with it, then trying to work with partner with them at this level will be a real drag (and probably not successful in the long run).

Has worked successfully with a virtual team in the past

You want to work with a business owner who has successfully worked with a virtually-based team already, and ideally has at least one contractor (usually a VA) in place. Often they will have worked with a VA (or two or more), a website designer, perhaps a copywriter, bookkeeper, etc. Any business that has created a solid foundation has usually done so with the efforts of more than just one person.

If a business owner has either a) never worked with a virtually-based team or b) has had bad experiences working with a virtual team and hasn't been able to make it work, these could be red flags. Before engaging with this client I would want to explore the reasons for this a bit further.

It could be that they have simply been doing it all on their own and may need some guidance on how to start hiring and delegating (which an OBM can help with). Or it could be that there are some serious control and/or delegation issues at play here that have made it impossible for the business owner to work effectively with anyone. As we already discussed, the "control freak" client is hard to work with, especially at the OBM level.

They are ready to let go and share

The business owner needs to be in a place where they are ready to let go of some things in order to allow their business to grow. Without an OBM in place your client is most likely the one who is managing their current team members and plugged into their day-to-day activities. For most, it is a bit of a journey to let go of these day-to-day things and trust that their OBM will take care of it for them.

You also want to ensure that they are open to the option of incentive-based pay, which is about sharing the wealth. Some business owners think this is great and really love the idea of having someone invested in their business at this level. Others may be totally new to the idea and could take a bit of time to warm up to the idea. Then there are business owners who say, "No way!" right off the bat, in which case they may not be a suitable OBM client for you.

They get what their role is as the leader/CEO of their company

This is probably one of the most important areas to explore with a potential client. What is their role as the business owner versus your role as the OBM? What expectations do they have of you as an OBM, and are those reasonable and achievable (as outlined in our previous chapters)? The business owner needs to stay plugged into a few key areas of their business, such as marketing (bringing in new business), development (new products and services) and leadership (providing the vision and heart of the business). Most anything outside of those areas can be delegated to the OBM.

Beware of the business owner who wants to give it all to their OBM!

You will come across some business owners who say they want to just "leave it all to my team so I can go sit on the beach somewhere." In my experience, this is a pipe dream more often than it is a reality. A business owner who wants to totally unplug themselves from their business needs to take a good long look at their situation. If they really don't want to be involved, maybe they need to sell the business instead of trying to hire someone to take it over for them. It's not fair or realistic for a business owner to just hand their business to someone and say, "Here you go, make me some money."

Online Business Manager Client Assessment and Intake Form

Here is a set of questions that we use when talking to potential OBM clients. The purpose is to ensure that the client is truly ready to hire an OBM and to see if there is compatibility for us to work together.

Feel free to use, tweak or add to this list as you see fit when talking to potential clients. I've added some notes for each question in *italics*.

1. Tell me about your business. What is your vision? Why did you start your business?

How passionate is the person about their business? Do they have a big vision? Can you feel the "energy" of their business when they are talking? Or are they kinda blah or dull? You want to look for someone who is really "plugged in" to their business – you can hear in their voice how excited and passionate they are.

2. Who is your target or niche market?

Does the person have a clearly defined niche market, or a group of people with similar challenges or interests that you can market to? Be aware if they are not clear on their niche market as they may need to do more work there before you start working with them.

3. What is your current revenue level? How steady is your income?

You may hesitate to ask this question as it can seem 'nosy', but it is essential that you know their revenue before you consider working with them. We've seen too many OBMs skip this question and assume the client was ready based on everything else, only to find out that they weren't in the 6+ figure range yet and therefore not ready for an OBM yet!

4. What is your business model? What are you selling? What is your current 'path to money' or outline of your business funnel, with details at each level.

You want to come away with a clear picture of exactly how they make their money – what are they selling, who is buying it and how do all their products and services fit together. This ties into question 3 – do they have a proven business model that is providing a steady level of income, or are they still struggling a bit to make ends meet?

5. What are your business goals for the next 6 months? Next 12 months? What do you want to accomplish?

Have they given some thought to what they want to accomplish in the next year or in the next five years? This is important – if they don't know yet what THEY want, you won't be able to help them get it. If they aren't clear on this yet they may need to hire a coach or business planning expert to help them create their goals. Also, are their goals achievable, e.g., creating four new products (feasible) versus becoming 'the next Tony Robbins' in 12 months (probably not going to happen)?

6. Who is currently on your team? What do they do for you?

It's important to know who is already on the team, including those who do ongoing work for them (e.g., VAs,) and contractors (web designers, social media experts, etc.). Most clients have several people on their team and are looking for an OBM to help coordinate and manage all the pieces (which of course we do!).

SIDENOTE

If they don't already have anyone on their team be aware that they will expect YOU to be the doer, even if they are hiring you as the OBM.

---

7. Where are the 'gaps' on your team? Are there any big challenges with your current team?

There must be gaps, otherwise why would they want to hire an OBM? You also want to know what any current challenges or issues are with their team so that you can come in ready to deal appropriately with a given situation.

8. Why do you want to hire an OBM? What could an OBM do for you?

What are their expectations of an OBM? Do you think you could provide what they are looking for? Or does it sound like they are looking for another kind of professional (e.g., a marketing expert). Ensure that their expectations aren't out of line with what you know you are able to provide.

Again, you want to keep an eye out for a business owner who just wants to abdicate their own role and turn everything over to the OBM.

9. How willing are you to delegate? What is your experience with delegating and what kind of communication do you require to feel good about trusting your delegate?

This is SO important to clarify with a potential client. A huge part of working as an OBM with a new client is building the trust factor. You need to know what makes THEM feel they can trust a team member, and how or if they've been burned in the past.

Many business owners aren't good at delegation, being that they start out as solopreneurs doing everything themselves. The chances are good that they may have some challenges with delegation and "letting go" of certain aspects of their business. It is the OBMs role to help them grow through this over time, as trust is built.

10. What questions do you have about the OBM role?

A good signal that a client is ready for an OBM are questions like:

> *— What will the compensation be?*
> *— Can we start out on one project first, to test our chemistry and work style?*

This is a great opportunity to really clarify the role of an OBM, particularly if the client is new to the idea of working with someone in this capacity. This is also a good time to talk about potential projects and clarify the difference between what you do as an OBM versus what a VA does.

Optional Questions, but still good to ask:

11. How often does your current business encounter emergencies or last-minute tasks?

Beware of a business owner who is constantly "'in crisis"!! This kind of chaotic and last-minute environment quite often comes from the personality of the business owner and can be tough to work within or change.

This can sometimes be hard to see during an initial conversation. Quite often you may not see chaos rear its ugly head until you jump in and do a project or two together.

12. How much documentation or work process is already in place? Do you have a standard operating procedures guide or customer service policies?

If they do have documentation in place already, great! If not, this can be a great starting point or a first project to work on with a potential new client, since these pieces are essential for sustained growth.

13. How much time off do you take in a year?

This can be telling as to what kind of work ethic and expectation they have. If they work 24/7, never see their kids, haven't been on vacation for years and are about to get divorced, this is something to explore. It could simply mean that they REALLY need to hire an OBM to help take the load off, or it could mean that they are addicted to their work and may expect the same from an OBM (yipes!).

CHAPTER 12

WHERE THE RUBBER MEETS THE ROAD - GETTING STARTED WITH YOUR CLIENTS

Don't Get Married on the First Date

I like to say – somewhat tongue in cheek – that working as an OBM for your clients is much like a marriage. Both parties need to be committed to the business and each other for the partnership to work and the business to grow.

And so just like we do when considering a life partner, you want to "date" your potential OBM clients before you commit to working with each other. This is to ensure that there is compatibility in the working relationship, so that you can have a strong and long-lasting business relationship.

The first date

Let's say you've talked to a potential new client and have determined that they are ready for and could use the services of an OBM. Start with a "get to know you" project, something that doesn't require any serious long-term commitment but that will still be of value to the client (versus a "make work" kind of project).

The project itself could be anything. I like to ask the client, "What has been on your wish list for quite some time now that you haven't been able to complete or get to?" This could be something like helping them launch a new training program or putting together a Standard Operating Procedures (SOP) guide. As I've mentioned earlier, helping to create an SOP can be a great first date project, as it gives you the chance to get to know your client's business and see how things are being done (and how they can be improved!).

It doesn't really matter what you do for a first date project, what matters is that you get a real snapshot of what is going on in their business and what it is like to work together. Is communication smooth and enjoyable or are you struggling to connect with the client? Is the business owner willing to answer your questions or do they expect you to just figure it all out on your own? Is the business really making money or is the reality of their business a bit different than what they shared up front? Most importantly, are you having fun?

As they say in marriage, don't get married expecting that you will be able to fix the other person after the wedding. If you are struggling with the business owner in any way during the dating stage, you may want to seriously consider whether you want to be their OBM. You should be able to tell after a few "dates" if this is someone that you would want to work with at the OBM level.

If everything goes great, you are excited by what the business is doing and you're having fun, then this could be a great OBM client. If you aren't having any fun and just aren't clicking with the business owner, then I highly recommend that you say no. Personality and communication styles are important at this level, and it could be that there is simply someone else out there who is a better fit for their business (and more ideal clients out there for you as well!).

You need to earn it (and so do they)

The OBM role is something that is earned by both the OBM and the business owner.

This is what the dating process is about – both parties getting to know each other and proving to each other who they are, what they stand for and what they are capable of. It is through the dating process that you earn the right to take on the OBM role. You are demonstrating that you have the attitude and skills that we talked about earlier (such as a marketing mindset and project management skills).

Likewise, the client is proving to you that they themselves and their business are truly ready to take it up a notch with the support of an OBM.

What I recommend to business owners is that they let their OBM **earn the role.** It could be someone new who starts with a few dating projects (as already discussed) or it could be someone within their existing team who has the attitude, aptitude and desire to grow into this role (and I'll share more on that next).

Incentive-based pay is something that MUST be earned. Although I am a huge fan of incentive-based pay, it is generally not something that you can include in the dating process. (You wouldn't open a joint bank account on the first date, would you?)

Start first with hourly retainer or project-based rates, and then when both you and your client have proven yourselves to each other and have made a commitment then **you earn the right to share in the wealth** of a growing business.

Don't forget to let a potential client know upfront that as an OBM you will be asking for an incentive-based payment plan. After you've worked together and have identified a long-term fit, you can then discuss an incentive-based plan that will work for all concerned.

Transitioning to an OBM role with current clients

Your current clients may be ripe and ready for an OBM, and who better for the role than someone who already knows them and their business!

First, you want to make sure that they fit the readiness criteria in the previous chapter. It could be that some of your clients aren't quite there yet, in which case you just want to stay tuned for when they are ready. Be especially careful that you don't try to impose the OBM role on a business that isn't ready yet, even if you love the client and are keen to help them grow their business. Prematurely taking on the role of OBM will put a lot of undue pressure on you and the business and could make an existing client relationship fall apart.

The journey for many VAs who have transitioned is that they first take a look at their client list to decide a) who is ready and b) who they enjoy working with the most. This is a good opportunity for you to let go of those that aren't your ideal clients and focus on working for a few that you enjoy the most.

The first step is to have a conversation with your clients about becoming their OBM. Let them know that you are making a change in your business to work with business owners at this level and that you would really love to explore this option with them since you enjoy working with them so much. Tell them about the role and how it is different from what you've been doing already. Let them know that you are excited to shift into the focus of growing their business versus just "doing stuff" in their business.

Several years ago my friend Cindy Greenway had this conversation with one of her long-time clients. "I scheduled a phone call with my client to let him know that I was making a change in my business. I shared how I was streamlining to work with just a few clients, and that I wanted him to be one of those clients. He was excited to have me shift into a more dedicated role. Being that we had already worked together for a few years, he knew that I was committed to seeing his business grow. He also recognized that he couldn't do it all alone and was quite happy to have someone help him out at this level."

After coming to agreement on her new role, Cindy took on more responsibility in her client's business. "I started managing all his websites, making sure content was up to date and coordinating with our web designers. I also took over managing event promotions and coordination."

It wasn't long after this that her client came to her with a specific request: "Cindy, I need you to step up and lead a specialized team and support our growing list of clients – holding their hand through our process and consulting with them to support their firm's growth". At first Cindy wasn't so sure she wanted to step into this expanded role, but her client persisted and today Cindy has a very visible role in the company, building connections, managing a team and consulting with the company's clients. It's been about 12 years since the initial conversation that grew the relationship and business is thriving.

You will also want to talk to them about shifting into an incentive-based payment plan. This is a new concept to most clients, so don't be surprised if they are a bit resistant to the idea at first. You may want to suggest that you give it a try with one project first and see how it goes.

My friend Erin has a great example of how you can start being paid on incentive. One of her clients was launching a paid training program and she approached her with an offer. Being that her client would usually get about 30 people to join with her existing marketing methods, Erin proposed to her that if she helped her get more than 30 people to join the program, she would earn a percentage of the revenue. Her client was open to the idea and thrilled to have Erin so committed to her project. They ended up getting more than 60 people in the program which meant more money for both the business owner and for Erin.

If your client is excited about having you become their OBM, then away you go! Make sure to set up a new agreement that reflects your new responsibilities along with your new incentive package.

The actual transition itself can take some time and is generally a matter of continually taking things off your client's plate and delegating to or hiring new team members to take all the "doing" off your plate as well.

CHAPTER 13

IT'S ALL UP TO YOU – CREATING SUCCESS ON YOUR OWN TERMS

"Faith is taking the first step even when you don't see the whole staircase."
- Martin Luther King, Jr.

What does success mean to you?

I find this to be such a fascinating question. When asked this question most people will at first say the usual things – making good money, finding a great relationship, having a nice house, going on vacation, etc. These are all worthy goals, but in and of themselves they generally don't bring the "feeling" of success along with them. How often do you hear of the person who has it all but is still miserable? It's an all too common story in today's day and age.

Success is much more about the feelings behind the "stuff" – what does it mean to you and your life to make more money? How will finding a great relationship add to your life? Why do you really want a nice house?

We've all heard the saying, "Be careful what you wish for, 'cause you just might get it!" It is REALLY important to look at what you want in life, and to truly understand **why you want it**. Otherwise you may get what you wish for, and realize that it doesn't matter to you or, in some cases, is a deterrent in your life.

For example, you could say "I want to make good money so that I don't have to worry about being able to pay my bills each month. I don't want to waste my energy on the negative and draining emotion of worry. I want to be able to focus that energy on having fun with my family instead."

Making money is the result, which really allows you to have more fun and light energy to share with your family. So the real success is not the money, it is the freedom of worry.

Once you are clear on what it is you want and why, then **the next step is to ask for it.**

If you *ask* for specific results in your business (and life), chances are that you will achieve these results.

Let me share the story of how I **unintentionally** got started working as an Online Business Manager.

In the summer of 2002, my husband and I had sold our condo and were in the process of building a house. There was a period between when we had to move out of our condo and when we could move into our house, so we spent a few months living with some friends. During this time, we also had to somehow find another $5,000 for the remainder of the down payment on our new house, or else we would lose the house and essentially be homeless. On top of all of this, I had just quit my job to focus on my new coaching practice, which was not making much money yet.

I distinctly remember one night lying in bed and wondering how the heck we were going to get the extra $5,000 we needed for our new house. I REALLY didn't want to go back to a job. There were no possibilities that I could think of, and so I simply put it out to the universe. I said, "All right, universe, here is the situation: We need to get an extra $5,000 in the next few months, and here's what I'm willing to do for that money." I wasn't sure what I was even looking for, but I did have a list of criteria which included working from home, having flexible hours and preferably in the coaching industry.

I kid you not, the very next day I received an email from Andrea, who at the time was General Manager of CoachVille.com, a large coach membership and training organization. Her and I been in touch a few times on a couple of volunteer projects, and she was looking to hire someone part-time to work for CoachVille. The number of hours and the rate worked out to be EXACTLY the amount of money that we needed for the rest of our down payment.

Let's just say I jumped on the opportunity, literally. And when I stopped jumping up and down for joy, I accepted the work and took this important first step in my virtual business. Not only did I get some wonderful experience working for CoachVille (trial by fire, I like to say), I made some great connections that have continued to this day.

The key point here is this – **I was VERY clear about what I wanted.** I was committed to being able to work from home. I knew exactly how much money I needed to make within a set time frame. And I really wanted to work in the industry that means the most to me – coaching.

And I wasn't afraid to ask for it, even though I honestly had no clue how or even if it would come about.

Although I didn't know it at the time, I was applying the principles of the Law of Attraction.

I consider the Law of Attraction to be the process of "let go and let God." Regardless of how you define God (higher power, universe, etc.), the Law of Attraction applies to everyone, and is a matter of getting clear on what you want, asking for it, being open to how it may show up in your life and taking action when it does.

Are you ready to play a bigger game?

I invite you to think big for your business and your life. Uncomfortably big, if you dare.

You may not know yet how to accomplish these big goals but go ahead and set the intention and see what possibilities show up.

To get you started on the process, take a few moments now and answer the following questions. If you aren't yet 100% sure on the answers, you may want to come back to this section later. Maybe take a day off and go enjoy some time in nature – being relaxed can really help open possibilities.

1. How many hours a week do you want to work in your business? Include all billable and non-billable time and be realistic. In a perfect world, we could all work two hours a week, but most of us will need to work at least 20 or more billable hours in a week to make any kind of decent income.

2. Putting aside the notion of "time for money," how much revenue would you like to bring in with your business? Again, be realistic but dare to dream here a bit. Don't settle for the amount you think you can make. Go ahead and ask for more, the "how" will come later.

3. What are you willing to do to make this money? What are you NOT willing to do? Be as specific as possible, based on your experience to date. For example, if you have a family, you may not be willing to travel. You also may not be able to make phone calls on behalf of your clients, if you're like me and you have a delightfully chatty 2-year-old at home with you.

4. How will having your dream business make you feel? This may seem silly at first, but this is perhaps the most important question of all. Getting in touch with the feelings around your business is often the most crucial catalyst for making things happen. And if your goals don't inspire any strong feelings, then you need to revisit them.

More than 'just an assistant'

I worked in a support role of some kind for the first five years after graduating from college. Two years as an Accounts Payable clerk, one year as an Executive Assistant, and then two years as a Marketing Coordinator.

All that time I always knew I wanted to do and be more than an assistant. Don't get me wrong, I absolutely respect and quite enjoy the role of the assistant. But for me it was a position that allowed me to hide behind whomever I was working for. I could play around a bit, do my work and not really have to stretch too much or take any risks. I worked for some great people and had some great experiences but the desire for more was always still there.

In 1999 I had the opportunity to go to work for a start-up web-based publications company. The owner Rob, who became a very good friend of mine, was a passionate and talented young man who was ready to go out and "grab life by the balls" (this was the tagline for the company). When he offered me a position with his start-up business I left my safe and cushy corporate job to take on the challenge. Scary, indeed, but I felt the calling and had to go for it.

That venture introduced me to the world of working online (which was in its infancy back then) and started me on the path to where I am today.

My goal for this book is to acknowledge that desire for others out there who may be ready for more. From the VA who is about to burst to the professional who feels trapped in their corporate job, there is a big world of opportunity for online based professionals. It may not be apparent to you yet, but if you have the desire for more then you have already taken the first step. I would be absolutely honoured if this book has provided you some inspiration and guidance for continuing the journey to make your dreams come true.

No great thing is accomplished alone, and I look forward to sharing this journey with you.

Learn more and come join us at www.CertifiedOBM.com.

THE OBM TOOLBOX

Visit www.OBMToolbox.com for a list of tools, resources and tips to get started on your OBM journey.

Go to www.CertifiedOBM.com for information on becoming a Certified OBM®.

Questions or comments? Email support@tinaforsyth.com to reach a member of my team.

ABOUT THE AUTHOR

Tina Forsyth

Tina Forsyth is a leadership and growth expert for service providers who have big missions and want to take their already successful business to the next level. She writes weekly on the topic of business and leadership growth on her website at www.TinaForsyth.com.

Having worked online since 1999, Tina Forsyth is a 'jill of all trades' when it comes to running and growing a profitable service-based business. She is the author of the award-winning book The Entrepreneur's Trap (available on Amazon) and creator of the CEO Business School for Transformational Leaders where she teaches entrepreneurs how to break free from busy and hire the right support (including OBMs!) so that they can create a business that doesn't rely solely on them.

Tina also founded the International Association of Online Business Managers and is the creator of the Certified OBM® Training– the only program of its kind to train high-end virtual managers. Learn more at: www.CertifiedOBM.com.

CONTRIBUTORS

Sharon Broughton

Sharon Broughton started her VA career in 2002 and after eight years of working with 6 and 7-figure businesses she became a Certified OBM® in 2010 and Infusionsoft Certified Partner in 2011. Sharon and her expert team work with clients on their online marketing strategy and implementation. As a Certified OBM® Trainer, Sharon is thrilled to be able to pass on her experiences and knowledge to VAs who are ready to take on this bigger role.

Keldie Jamieson

Keldie Jamieson started her online business in 2009 offering project, operations, and financial management, business startup, marketing, and event services. She blended over 30 years of corporate expertise with online business management training to become a Certified OBM® in 2011. As a Certified OBM Trainer, Keldie is now training and mentoring others to transition their corporate world experience into a successful business and career.

Sarah Noked

Sarah Noked is an MBA graduate, Certified OBM® and Digital Marketing Strategist with more than 10 years' business experience. Sarah and her OBM team help clients stay on track through project, team, launch and operations management. As a Certified OBM® Trainer, Sarah is working with other OBMs and VAs looking to scale and grow profitable teams and businesses.

Made in the USA
Lexington, KY
19 October 2018